Learning Language Arts Through Literature

THE PURPLE TEACHER BOOK

By

Debbie Strayer

and

Susan Simpson

Common Sense Press

The *Learning Language Arts Through Literature* series:

The Blue Book - 1st Grade Skills
The Red Book - 2nd Grade Skills
The Yellow Book - 3rd Grade Skills
The Orange Book - 4th Grade Skills
The Purple Book - 5th Grade Skills
The Tan Book - 6th Grade Skills
The Green Book - 7th Grade Skills
The Gray Book - 8th Grade Skills
The Gold Book - World Literature - High School Skills
The Gold Book - American Literature - High School Skills
The Gold Book - British Literature - High School Skills

Copyright ©1998 by:
Common Sense Press, Inc.
8786 Highway 21
Melrose, FL 32666
www.commonsensepress.com

Printed in the United States of America.

Rev 08/15
Printed 08/15
ISBN 978-1-880892-85-5

Introduction

     As parents we watched and marveled at the way our little ones learned to talk. By listening and responding to English spoken well, they were able to communicate quite clearly. The process was so gradual that they were not even aware it was taking place.

     It is the belief of those associated with the *Learning Language Arts Through Literature* series that written language can best be learned in the same manner. By reading fine literature and working with good models of writing, children will receive a quality education in language arts. If you desire to teach using this integrated approach to language, this curriculum is for you.

     In her books, Dr. Ruth Beechick has confirmed that this method of teaching is an appropriate and successful way to introduce our students to the joys of reading, writing, and thinking. Our own experiences using these lessons with children have encouraged us to share them with you. Their enjoyment and enthusiasm for reading and writing is an unmatched recommendation for this method of teaching.

     The **integrated language approach** has the benefits of all teaching methods. By working with pieces of literature, you focus on grammar, vocabulary, writing, reading, spelling, penmanship, and thinking skills. Your student has the best advantage for learning skills in this effective and lasting manner.

     Grammar is taught in conjunction with writing, not as an isolated subject. Your student's **vocabulary** will be enhanced by reading the good literature selections which have been carefully chosen for his grade level. We realize that every student functions at a different reading level. For the more hesitant reader, we recommend you, the teacher, read aloud with your student. Grade appropriate **reading skills** are included. Helpful **Spelling Tips** are included to help your student develop his spelling skills. **Penmanship** skills may be developed as your student writes his dictation or any other writing assignment. Handwriting is influenced by maturity of fine motor ability so the goal is to improve from the point at which your student begins. **Thinking skills** are developed throughout the activities in this manual. Anytime a student is asked to respond to the literature with discussion, writing, drawing, or completing an activity, your student is developing higher order thinking skills.

How to Use This book

This book provides materials, activities, and suggestions that will encourage and benefit you and create a learning environment for your student. Since everyone is different, we suggest that you try our ideas and then freely experiment until you find patterns that work for you.

Let us first introduce *Learning Language Arts Through Literature*. After this introduction you will find the following:

Book Studies

There are four book studies contained in this teacher's manual. Each *Book Study* is conveniently placed prior to the *Everyday Words* which use the literature passages from the book. Sometimes a *Book Study* which relates to the particular unit will precede it. You may complete the *Book Study* in a week prior to the *Everyday Words* lessons. If your student needs more time, adjust your schedule accordingly. Or you may choose to complete the *Book Study* throughout three to four weeks as you work through the *Everyday Words* lessons. The four *Book Study* units are provided for your student's enjoyment of good literature. Each story has convenient summary, listed with the readability level. Be flexible in how you use the book units. If you know your student is a good reader and comprehends well, you may choose to ask only certain questions. For your hesitant reader, use the questions to help you discuss the book. Do not make this a tedious task, but rather use it as a springboard for your student to tell you about the story.

Everyday Words

Each lesson found in this section contains a passage of literature and learning activities. These activities are designed to help your student learn language skills in their context while developing writing and thinking skills. An emphasis is placed on grammar skills appropriate for fifth grade. In most of the lessons, the student will either copy the passage or write it from dictation.

Copying material is a very powerful learning activity. It trains a student to look for details, strive for accuracy, and learn to write. After the student has made his first copy, ask him to check it with the model found in the *Student Activity Book* and make any necessary corrections. When dictation is used in the lesson, the passage will need to be read clearly, sentence by sentence. It is also important to you use your voice to stress pauses and indicate punctuation marks.

Since this method may be new for you, here are a few suggestions:

1. Before dictation or copying, read the entire passage to your student.
2. Begin the dictation by reading one sentence at a time. If necessary, repeat the sentence, reading it one phrase at a time.
3. Instruct your student to leave a blank space between each line so that corrections are easy to make.
4. After dictation or copying, allow your student to use the passage to edit the work. At first have the student check his work one line at a time. Asking the student to correct the work all at once may prove to be frustrating.

Review Activities

Review Activities are found directly after each *Everyday Words*. New skills taught in each lesson are included in the *Review Activities*. It is not necessary to do each activity. Choose the skills your student needs.

Assessments

Interspersed among the lessons in *The Purple Book* you will find assessments. Easy-to-use and administer, these tools help you assess the progress of your student. The goal of the assessments is to obtain information about your student's progress in order to determine how you, the teacher, can better assist your student.

An I C.A.N. Assessment has been created for each *Book Study* and *Unit*. At this grade level, you can expect your student to complete his work neatly with a good attitude. You may use these assessments to grade your student accordingly.

Skills Index

The *Language Arts Skills Index* is located in the back of the manual. To ensure that skills commonly held appropriate for fifth grade instruction were adequately covered, much research was involved in the writing of this book. This information was primarily gleaned from these sources:

You CAN Teach Your Child Successfully by Ruth Beechick
Teaching Children: A Curriculum Guide to What Children Need to Know at Each Level Through Sixth Grade by Diane Lopez

If your child has a particularly strong or weak area, you can easily locate lessons that will address specific skills using the skills index. If your child receives standardized testing, skills listed on the test may also be found in the skills index.

Enrichment Activities

In each lesson you will find the treasure chest icon for the *Enrichment Activities*. This is your cue to look for the activity located in the *Student Activity Book* where they are listed in full. Answers to these activities are found in the back of this manual. While optional, these activities develop thinking and reasoning skills necessary for higher level learning.

Bibliography

Next you will find the Bibliography. This will give you all the information you need to locate the books quoted in the lessons. The selection includes wonderful books that we hope your family will read and enjoy.

Materials To Use

To use the manual you will need pencils, paper, colored pencils, drawing paper, a notebook, file folders, and construction paper. Additional materials are listed in the beginning of each lesson. Frequently in the lessons, the student must find a book he is familiar with, so children's books (either your own books or library books) are needed from time to time.

Previous lessons are often used again, so keep all the student's work until the entire unit is completed.

Reference books, such as a dictionary and thesaurus, will be used as well as encyclopedias. Availability of these materials in either the home or library is adequate.

Student Activity Books

Student Activity Books are available for your student. Daily exercises corresponding to each lesson are included for easy use.

Table of Contents

BOOK STUDY

on

Farmer Boy

Skills

Vocabulary
Reading Comprehension
Sequencing Events

Farmer Boy
Written by Laura Ingalls
Wilder
Published by Harper
Collins

Readability - 5th grade

Introducing
Farmer Boy

Spark:
You may already know about Laura Ingalls and *The Little House* series. This is a story about her husband-to-be, Almanzo, when he was a young boy.

Summary

Almanzo lives with his parents, his brother, Royal, and his sisters, Eliza Jane and Alice. The Wilder family lived in New York state in the mid 1800s. For his ninth birthday, he receives a calf-yoke and a sled. He is now old enough to break a calf, but his dream is to break a colt.

Everyone has chores that help the family run smoothly. On Saturdays, Mother bakes all day, and evening is bath time. Sundays are special days; breakfast is deliciously stacked pancakes, and everyone dresses up and goes to church. On Sundays, there is no working or playing.

Winter brings about ice cutting. The ice is stored carefully in sawdust so they can have ice cream all summer. After the snow melts, there is spring cleaning and planting. The summer is filled with long hours of hard work harrowing and weeding the fields. Fall brings about the harvest and the County Fair.

These are some life experiences through Almanzo's eyes. He learns about integrity and hard work from his father. When Father sees Almanzo's maturity and good sense, he gives him Starlight, the family colt.

Vocabulary

Find the word in its context. Reread the sentences before and after the word. Do you understand the meaning of the word? Now, look up the word in the dictionary and write a clear, simple definition, and use it in a sentence.

1. petrified (Chapter "Winter Evening")

2. geraniums (Chapter "Birthday")

3. cultivate (Chapter "Summer-Time")

4. reaping (Chapter "Early Harvest")

5. apprentice (Chapter "The Little Bobsled")

Complete the following sentences with the correct vocabulary word.

OR

Write your own sentences using the vocabulary words.

1. The farmers began _____ the crops.

2. The _____ piece of wood decorated the mantle.

3. The carpenter's _____ learned how to craft fine furniture.

4. The pot of _____ looked beautiful on the window sill.

5. Father will _____ the potatoes tomorrow.

1. hardened

2. a plant usually with pretty red blossoms and velvety green leaves
3. to prepare land for growing
4. harvesting

5. a helper

1. reaping

2. petrified

3. apprentice

4. geraniums

5. cultivate

1. Almanzo thought Bill and the other big boys were going to beat up Mr. Corse. Mr. Corse knew of Bill Ritchie's plans and came prepared. He beat the boys with Almanzo's father's whip.

2. In those days, jobs had to be done as required. Often, school took second place after chores.

3. Although it was nice to take a break from chores, Sundays meant no working and no playing. Sundays were spent being quiet. It was difficult for Almanzo to remain inactive for so long. Chores would be better, he thought.

4. The whip was used to make a loud, cracking sound to train his calves. He knew the best way to have hard working, good-natured oxen was to be patient and gentle. He wanted Star and Bright to trust him.

5. The potatoes were cut into pieces, with each piece containing two or three eyes. Almanzo and Alice dropped the pieces of potato, and Royal and Father followed them and covered them with dirt.

Discussion Questions

Chapters 1 – 4

1. What did Almanzo think Bill Ritchie was going to do to Mr. Corse? (Chapter 4)

   What happened instead? (Chapter 4)

Chapters 5 – 7

2. Almanzo's father said that he and Royal could stay home from school to help with the ice cutting. Why do you think Father allowed the boys to miss school? (Chapter 5)

Chapters 8 – 10

3. At the end of chapter 8, it says that Almanzo is glad when it is time to do his chores. Why do you think so?

4. Father helped Almanzo make a whip. What was it used for? Why did Almanzo never whip his calves? (Chapter 9)

Chapters 11 – 12

5. Explain how the Wilders planted potatoes. (Chapter 11)

Chapters 13 – 15

6. Mother was nervous about having money in her house. Where were all the places she hid the money? (Chapter 13)

Chapters 16 – 18

7. How did Almanzo get his half dollar? (Chapter 16)

8. What was Almanzo going to do with his half dollar? (Chapter 16)

Chapters 19 – 21

9. Almanzo won first prize for his pumpkin at the County Fair. He thought perhaps he had cheated by feeding his pumpkin milk. Do you think he cheated? (Chapter 21)

Chapters 22 – 26

10. Christmas dinner was a delicious feast for Almanzo. Describe your favorite meal in detail. (Chapter 26)

Chapters 27 – 29

11. Why do you think Father gave Starlight to Almanzo? (Chapter 29)

6. **She hid it in the pantry, the linen-closet, under Father's socks in the drawers, and under her pillow.**

7. **Frank dared Almanzo to ask his father for a nickel. Almanzo took the dare, but Father ended up giving him a half dollar.**

8. **He was going to buy a sucking pig to raise.**

9. **No. Allow discussion.**

10. **Answers will vary.**

11. **Almanzo had shown responsibility with his calves and had begun to understand the value of hard work.**

1.

a. **Bill Ritchie's gang plans an attack on Mr. Corse.**

b. **Almanzo gets a sled for his birthday.**

c. **Almanzo slips into the icy water during ice sawing time.**

d. **The Wilder family sells five hundred bushel of potatoes.**

e. **Father and Mother go on vacation to Uncles Andrew's.**

2.

a. **An exploding potato hurts Almanzo's eye.**

b. **Almanzo's pumpkin gets a blue ribbon at the Fair.**

c. **Almanzo receives a jack-knife in his Christmas stocking.**

d. **Almanzo returns the pocketbook to Mr. Thompson.**

e. **Father gives Starlight to Almanzo.**

Sequencing Events

1. Read the events from *Farmer Boy*. Number them in the order which they happened.

    a. The Wilder family sells five hundred bushels of potatoes.
    b. Bill Ritchie's gang plans an attack on Mr. Corse.
    c. Almanzo steps into the icy water during ice sawing time.
    d. Father and Mother go on vacation to Uncles Andrew's.

2. Read these events from *Farmer Boy* and number them in the order in which they happened.

    a. Father gives Starlight to Almanzo.
    b. Almanzo receives a jack-knife in his Christmas stocking.
    c. An exploding potato hurts Almanzo's eye.
    d. Almanzo returns the pocketbook to Mr. Thompson.
    e. Almanzo's pumpkin gets a blue ribbon at the Fair.

I C.A.N. Assessment

for

Farmer Boy - Book Study A

After the *Book Study* is completed, check off each **I C.A.N.** objective with your teacher.

—— **C** I can **complete** my work.

——   I can be **creative**.

—— **A** I can be **accurate**.

——   I can do my work with a good **attitude**.

—— **N** I can do my work **neatly**.

EVERYDAY WORDS

in
"America"

Skills
Dictionary
Homonym
Memorization
Meter
Noun
Poetry
Possessive Noun
Pronouns
Rhyme
Syllable

📝 **Teacher's Note:** As your student completes each lesson, choose skills from the Review Activities that he needs. The Review Activities follow each lesson.

"America"

My country, 'tis of thee,
Sweet land of liberty,
Of thee I sing;
Land where my fathers died,
Land of the Pilgrims' pride,
From every mountainside
Let Freedom ring.

"America", by Samuel Francis Smith, (1808-1895)

1. a. Listen as your teacher reads this poem to you. After your teacher reads it aloud a second time, look over the poem and list any words that are unfamiliar to you.

   Words are listed alphabetically in the dictionary. Most dictionaries have **guide words** on the top of each page. Guide words tell you the first and last word listed on a page. Learn to use these guide words to help you find your word quickly and easily. Look at the sample dictionary page in 2b. Look up any unfamiliar words in the dictionary, and write the definitions using your own words. After making sure you know the meaning of all the words, read this poem aloud to your teacher.

   b. List four to six words that you should study for spelling this week, or use the following list of suggested words: country, died, mountain, liberty.

   There are several words that are spelled with the same ending as *mountain*. We say /moun**ten**/ but it is spelled *moun**tain***.

Spelling Tip
Words like *mountain* are spelled
with **ain** to make
an **/en/** sound.

Copy the following words and underline **ain**. Say the words aloud as you write them.

fountain	captain	bargain
again	curtain	certain

c. This poem describes America in three ways. The descriptions are easy to find because they each include the word *land*. Find and circle three descriptions.

d. All of these descriptions talk about our heritage, or history. Talk with your teacher about the answer to these three questions regarding our history.

    1) From what do you think our country provided liberty?
    2) Who do you think the poem means by "my fathers?"
    3) According to the poem, what was the Pilgrims' attitude toward American?

e. Think about the ways Americans remember the events and people of our history. Write a list of ways we remember our beginnings as a nation and the people who have worked to helped establish our country. A **list** does not have to be complete sentences.

2. a. Words can be broken down into **syllables**. A syllable consists of one of the following:

a vowel sound
example: (**a** in *a*/*bout*)

a vowel sound with consonant sounds before it
example: (**fa** in *fa*/*thers*)

a vowel sound with consonant sounds after it
example: (**er** in *lib*/*er*/*ty*)

a vowel sound with consonant sounds surrounding it
example: (**dom** in *Free*/*dom*)

The key to finding syllables is to look for vowel sounds and determine what, if any, consonant sounds go with them. If you are unsure of how to divide a word into syllables, look in your dictionary. (See sample dictionary on page 12.)

1.
c. Sweet land of liberty.
Land where my fathers died.
Land of the Pilgrim's pride.

d. 1) Our country provided liberty from England's rule.
2) "My Fathers" mean the early Americans.
3) The Pilgrims felt pride toward America.

e. Independence Day
Thanksgiving
Williamsburg, etc.

Accented syllables are spoken with more stress than unaccented syllables. The word *chicken*, for example, has two separate vowel sounds, so there are two syllables. The consonants that go with the vowel sounds make the syllables *chick/en*. When we say *chicken*, the syllable *chick* is stressed or accented, but the *en* is soft. Therefore, the **accent** is on *chick* and *en* is unaccented. To show this, we use marks over the syllables that look like this: chićk ĕn. If you are unsure of where to place the accent, look in your dictionary.

b. Look at the sample dictionary page below. A dictionary gives you the following helpful information.

1) definition   2) syllabication
3) pronunciation/accent   4) part of speech
5) Some dictionaries give a sample sentence.

---

scorpion   secret

scorpion (skór pe en), noun: an arachnid with a poisonous sting
While cleaning the basement, the man was stung by a scorpion.

scout (skout), noun: one who is sent to spy
The scout reported back to his commander.
verb: to hunt to find something
Dad told me to scout for worms.

scream (skrem), verb: to make a loud piercing cry
I will scream for help.
noun: a loud piercing cry
The scream was heard throughout the neighborhood.

sea(se), noun: a body of salt water
The tourists sailed over the calm sea.

secret (sé krit), noun: knowledge kept unknown
She whispered a secret to her friend.
adjective: kept from being known
The boys found a secret passageway.

---

c. Look at each line of the first verse of "America," by Samuel Francis Smith. These lines can be divided into syllables, and the syllables can be marked accented or unaccented. First, count the number of syllables in each line. Next, mark the syllables accented or unaccented. Do you see a pattern? This pattern of accented and unaccented syllables is called **meter.**

d. Read the verse again, using the marks in your pronunciation guide. Read the accented syllables with greater emphasis than the unaccented syllables. It may sound very awkward at first, so practice reading several times.

3. a. Look at the first line of "America." Can you find the work that names a person, place, thing, or idea? A word that names a person, place, thing, or idea is called a **noun**.
   Ex: mailman – person   library – place
        chair – thing   anger – idea

b. Write two nouns for each of the following:
   1) person   2) place   3) thing

c. Words that name an idea are probably the hardest nouns to recognize. This is because an idea cannot be held or touched. The word *joy* is a noun. It cannot be touched but it is still an idea or thought; therefore, it is a noun. Some other nouns which express an idea are *war, flight, courage*, etc.

d. Write two nouns which express an idea.

e. Can you find three more nouns in "America" which name an idea?

f. Look at the second, fourth, and seventh lines of the literature passage and list all the nouns.

g. Look at line one of "America." To whom does the word *my* refer? Look at line three. To whom does the word *I* refer? Now, look at line four. To whom does the word *my* refer?

   Words like *my* and *I* take the place of a noun. These words are called **pronouns**.

---

2. c.
My coun try tis of thee, 6

Sweet land of liberty, 6

Of thee I sing, 4

Land where my fathers

died, 6

Land of the Pilgrim's pride, 6

From every mountainside, 6

Let Freedom ring, 4

✏ **Teacher's Note: Stress marks may vary according to how it is read.**

3.
a. country
b. Possible answers:
   1) boy, girl, police, soldier, baby, etc.
   2) park, store, home, lake, forest, etc.
   3) chair, car, rabbit, circus, food, etc.

d. Answers will vary. Refer to examples given.

e. liberty, pride, freedom

f. line 2-land, liberty
   line 4-land, father
   line 7-Freedom

g. *My* refers to the poet or person reciting the poem.
   I refers to the poet or person reciting the poem.

3.

h. John made *his* bed and ran downstairs. *He* ate breakfast and fed *his* dog.

i. 1) their
   2) them
   3) They
   4) his
   5) He

h. Look at the following sentence:

John made *John's* bed and ran downstairs. *John* ate breakfast and fed *John's* dog.

Does it sound funny? You use pronouns every day when you speak, but you use it so often and easily, you may not realize it. Rewrite the sentences, replacing the italicized words with the correct pronoun. Look at the Personal Pronoun Chart below if you need help.

i. Now, try replacing the italicized words with pronouns in these sentences:

1) Ron and Sandy fixed *Ron and Sandy's* bikes.
2) Alan waited for *Ron and Sandy*.
3) *Ron and Sandy* raced to the corner.
4) Alan got on *Alan's* bike to meet them.
5) *Alan* was glad to see them.

j. Review your spelling words.

PERSONAL PRONOUNS		
Singular		
Subjective	**Possessive**	**Objective**
I	my, mine	me
you	your, yours	you
he, she, it	his, her, hers, its	it, him, her
Plural		
Subjective	**Possessive**	**Objective**
we	our, ours	us
you	your, yours	you
they	their, theirs	them

4. a. Read the excerpt on page 15 from the book *Patriotic Songs*, part of the *Color the Classics* series. This excerpt tells about the song "America" and its author, Samuel Francis Smith. Answer the following questions.

1) Why do you think Samuel Francis Smith was interested in the ride of Paul Revere?
2) Where did Samuel go to college? What did he decide to do after college?
3) When did Samuel write "America?" When was it first performed?

b. Optional: Take an oral or written spelling pretest.

The Story of "America"
(My County, 'Tis of Thee)
Samuel Francis Smith, 1808-1895

Samuel Francis Smith was born in Boston, Massachusetts on October 21, 1808. He was an only child who developed a fascination with the patriotic history of our country.

One spring morning in 1815, the pastor of Christ Church began his sermon discussing the events of Paul Revere's ride to Lexington. Samuel often daydreamed about that heroic horse ride. He wondered what it would have been like to have traveled all those miles through the middle of the night. How did the British find out about Lexington? What was Paul Revere thinking as he crossed the Charles River? How fast was he riding? How long did it take him to get all the way to Lexington? Would he be caught? Would he ever see his family again? Oh, how Samuel wished he could have been there!

One day while waiting for his school friends, he happened to see the church maintenance man, Mr. Perry, sweeping the steps of Christ Church. Samuel asked him if he saw Paul Revere anymore. Perry mentioned that Paul was quite old now and that only his son, Joseph Revere, came to church. They sat and talked about the event that followed the hanging of the two lanterns. Perry described how Paul had to sneak past the British warship, the *Somerset*, in the channel and mount the horse that was waiting for him on the other side. Then Mr. Perry pulled out a set of old keys and said, "Come with me." Curiously, the boy followed the custodian up the stairs to the belfry. After opening the door, the two stood there looking at two old lanterns. One was broken. Samuel's eyes could not have widened any bigger. *"Are these…?"* *"Yes,"* said Mr. Perry, *"they certainly are!"*

Samuel's father had one dream for his only son. He wanted Samuel to attend Harvard University and receive a great education. Harvard was founded by men from England's University of

4. a.
1) Answers will vary.
2) Samuel went to Harvard. He then decided to become a pastor.
3) Samuel wrote America while translating music books from German to English for Lowell Mason. It was first performed on July 4, 1831.

Oxford and University of Cambridge. These Puritan men and their families believed that England's Universities were corrupt. Their intent was to establish a University in America with moral character, dependence upon scriptural principles and high academic standards. For many years Mr. Smith worked hard to make sure his son could attend that University. Eventually, his long hours as a cooper took their toll. When Samuel was 15, his father died unexpectedly. It was time to take care of his mother and fulfill his father's dream. Within a short time, Samuel was studying diligently at Harvard where he made many friends. Oliver Wendell Holmes and Lowell Mason were among his closest lifelong friends. Oliver Wendell Holmes and Lowell Mason were among his closest friends. Samuel quickly earned reputation as a linguist and a writer. He translated and wrote for newspapers and journals. Because he studied all day and all night, he eventually mastered Latin, Greek, German, as well as 11 other languages.

He graduated from Harvard in 1829. Samuel was asked by many what he was going to do with his life after college. He considered law, medicine, teaching and translating. After much prayer, he decided to enroll in Andover Theological Seminary to become a pastor.

In February of 1831, his first year at Andover, 24 year-old Samuel heard a loud knock on his door. There stood Lowell Mason, a popular musician, with an arm full of books. Lowell, who did not understand German, asked Smith to translate the music books from German to English. Lowell was looking for an appropriate piece of music that he could use with the children for the upcoming 4th of July celebration five months away. Samuel accepted the task and Lowell left.

Samuel came across a piece of music that instantly grabbed his attention. He took a scrap of paper from the wastebasket and quickly jotted down five stanzas in 30 minutes. Thinking he had better continue with the work that Lowell had just left him, he placed the wastepaper in one of the books and forgot all about it. Little did he realize that the words he adapted to the tune would become a national hymn and that the tune would be shared by both England (*God Save the King*) and America.

On July 4th of that same year, Samuel walked down to the annual celebration given by the children of the community. What a shock to see the children stand up, follow the music leader, Lowell Mason, and sing the five verses that he had completely forgotten. *"My verses,"* he exclaimed. After the performance was over, the applause was overwhelming. Even more thrilling was the young woman, Mary White Smith, who came up to congratulate him for such a beautiful poem. She later became Mrs. Samuel Smith.

Samuel preached in several large Baptist churches for many years. He composed over 150 hymns during his lifetime. Samuel always had a love for missions; he strongly promoted them. One of his sons became a missionary to Burma. When all his children were grown, he and Mary visited many countries as missionaries.

Annual Celebrations: Lowell wanted Smith to pick a melody from the collection of books and translate the German into English for the children's celebration. It was performed in Boston on July 4, 1831 at the Park Street Church. Smith did not know he was using "God Save the King." He was later accused of being pro-British. It became so popular that the tune was sung at patriotic rallies, schools and during the Civil War. One reason for its success was because people already knew the tune. There were originally five stanzas, but the last one was dropped because of its anti-British sentiment. The present four stanzas are exactly the way he wrote them. No revisions. The song was translated into Swedish, Latin, Italian and German. Once it became popular with the Americans, Samuel commented, "If only I had known that my song would be so well liked, I would have taken greater pains with it."

Used by permission from *Color the Patriotic Classics*.
One in the series of historical books and
musical cassette tapes form *Color the Classics* by Carmen Ziarkowski.

5. a. It is wonderful to memorize poetry. There are other things that are good to memorize as well, such as Scriptures. Memorizing something is not that hard, it just takes practice.

Begin memorizing "America." You will need to practice more than one time to remember it. The best way to remember is to practice for a few minutes a couple of times a day.

Tips for Memorizing Poetry

1. Read your poem silently.
2. Reread the first three lines, either silently or out loud.
3. Read the first three lines again out loud.
4. Now look away, or close your eyes, and repeat the first three lines.
5. If you get stuck, open your eyes, find the word you need and then go on to the end of those three lines.
6. Keep doing this until you feel sure you know them.

---

b. When you have the poem memorized, say it for your family or class. By now you may know that this is also a song, so you may want to sing it instead. Once you have presented it on your own (either by speaking or singing) ask everyone to join in and do it with you the second time.

c. When you have the poem memorized, say it for your family or class.

d. Take a spelling test.

e. Optional: Choose skills from the *Review Activities* on the next page.

Review Activities

Choose the skills your student needs to review.

1. *Accented Syllables*
Say the following words aloud. Place stress marks on the accented syllables.

   a. heaven
   b. surprise
   c. calendar
   d. fantastic
   e. carpenter
   f. united
   g. tremendous
   h. tornado
   i. towards
   j. paper

2. *Nouns*

   a. Write two nouns that name a person.
   b. Write two nouns that name a place.
   c. Write two nouns that name a thing.
   d. Write two nouns that name an idea.

3. *Pronouns*

   Replace the italicized words with the correct pronoun.

   a. Robert went to *Robert's* uncle's house.
   b. Uncle Tom wasn't home, but *Uncle Tom* left a message on the door.
   c. The message said that *Uncle Tom* had gone fishing.
   d. Robert joined *Uncle Tom* at the lake.
   e. Robert and *Uncle Tom* fished all day.

4. *Poetry Memorization*

   Recite the first verse of "America."

1.
a. heá ven
b. sur prise
c. cal en dar
d. fan tas tic
e. car pen ter
f. u ni ted
g. trem en dous
h. tor na do
i. to wards
j. pa per

2.
a. Answers will vary.
b. Answers will vary.
c. Answers will vary.
d. Answers will vary.

3.
a. Robert went to *his* uncle's house.
b. Uncle Tom wasn't home, but *he* left a message on the door.
c. The message said that *he* had gone fishing.
d. Robert joined *him* at the lake.
e. *They* fished all day.

4. Self Explanatory

📝 **Teacher's Note:** As your student completes each lesson, choose skills from the Review Activities that he needs. The Review Activities follow each lesson.

1.
a. Answers will vary.

📝 **Teacher's Note:** Some grammar books refer to these words as homophones.

"America"

(verse 4)
Our fathers' God, to Thee,
Author of liberty,
To Thee we sing;
Long may our land be bright
With Freedom's holy light;
Protect us by Thy might,
Great God, our King.

"America", by Samuel Francis Smith, (1808-1895)

1. a. In this verse of "America" there are many important words that describe what Americans believe. Two of these words are *liberty* and *freedom*. You may already know the meanings of these words or you may have looked them up in the dictionary in Lesson 1. Write a sentence using these words.

   b. List four to six words that you should study for spelling this week, or use the following list of suggested words: author, bright, with, protect.

   Some words spell the long **i** sounds with **igh**, as in *light*.

   ┌─────────────────────────────────────┐
   │   **Spelling Tip**   │
   │ Words like **light** with the long   │
   │ **/i/** sound are spelled with **igh.** │
   └─────────────────────────────────────┘

   Copy the following words and underline **igh**. Say the words aloud as you write them.

bright	flight	light	blight
might	slight	sight	tight
high	night	plight	right

   c. Look at the first word of verse 4 in "America." Say the word *our* aloud. Do you know of another word that sounds the same but has a different meaning and sometimes a different spelling? The word *hour* is pronounced the same, but has a different meaning and a different spelling. These words are called **homonyms.**

d. Find words from the literature passage to match the spelling homonyms.

1) grate   3) two   5) buy
2) mite   4) wee

e Citizenship in America assures us of certain freedoms like those described in the Bill of Rights. Read the Ten Amendments that make up the Bill of Rights. After reading them or listening as your teacher reads them, make a list of some of the freedoms we have as Americans.

f. Look over the list you made of the freedoms listed in the Bill of Rights. Choose one of the freedoms. Think about how your life would be different if that freedom was taken away. Write a two or three sentence description of how things would change.

Amendments to the Constitution

Amendment 1
Congress shall make no law respecting an establishment of religion, or prohibiting the free exercise thereof; or abridging the freedom of speech, or of the press; or the right of the people peaceable to assemble, and to petition the government for a redress of grievance.

Amendment 2
A well-regulated militia being necessary to the security of a free State, the right of the people to keep and bear arms shall not be infringed.

Amendment 3
No soldier shall, in time of peace, be quartered in any house without the consent of the owner; nor in time of war but in a manner to be prescribed by law.

Amendment 4
The right of the people to be secure in their person, houses, papers and effects, against unreasonable searches and seizures, shall not be violated, and no warrants shall issue but upon probable cause, supported by oath or affirmation, and particularly describing the place to the be searched, and the persons or things to be seized.

---

1. d.
   1) great
   2) might
   3) to
   4) we
   5) by

e. **Possible Answers:**
   freedom of worship
   freedom of speech and press
   the right to petition the government
   the right to a trial etc.

f. **Answers will vary.**

Amendment 5
No person shall be held to answer for a capital or otherwise infamous crime, unless on a presentment or indictment of a grand jury, except in cases arising in the land or naval forces, in the militia, when in actual service in time of war or public danger; nor shall any person be subject for the same offence to be twice put in jeopardy of life or limb; nor shall be compelled in any criminal case to be a witness against himself, nor deprived of life, liberty, or property, without due process of law; nor shall private property be taken for public use, without just compensation.

Amendment 6
In all criminal prosecutions the accused shall enjoy the right to a speech and public trial, by an impartial jury of the State and district wherein the crime shall have been committed, which district shall have been previously ascertained by law, and to be informed to the nature and cause of the accusation; to be confronted with the witnesses against him; to have compulsory process for obtaining witnesses in his favor and to have the assistance of counsel for his defense.

Amendment 7
In suits at common law, where the value in controversy shall exceed twenty dollars, the right of trial by jury shall be preserved, and no fact tried by jury shall be otherwise examined in any court of the United States than according to the rules of the common law.

Amendment 8
Excessive bail shall not be required, nor excessive fines imposed, nor cruel and unusual punishments inflicted.

Amendment 9
The enumeration in the Constitution of certain rights shall not be construed to deny or disparage others retained by the people.

Amendment 10
The powers not delegated to the United States by the Constitution, nor prohibited by it to the States, are reserved to the States respectively, or the people.

2. a. Read this sentence: This is the boy's book.

   To whom did the book belong?

   The word *boy's* is a possessive noun. A **possessive noun** is usually written with an apostrophe and **s** (**'s**).

   b. Look at the fifth line of the poetry verse. Write the possessive noun. Did you remember the apostrophe and **s** (**'s**)?

   c. Read each sentence and fill in the blanks.
      Ex: I walked to my *friend's house*.
           The <u>house</u> belongs to my <u>friend</u>.

      1) Where are your *brother's keys*?
         The _____ belong to _____.
      2) Give me the *dog's* dish.
         The _____ belongs to _____.
      3) Look at the *bird's nest*.
         The _____ belongs to _____.

   d. Each of the sentences in **2c** tell us about a noun that belongs to someone or something. There is only one owner, so we call these **singular possessive nouns**. Using your name, write three sentences telling about things that belong to you. Use an apostrophe and **s** (**'s**) to show that the things belong to you.
      Ex: Mrs. Strayer's hair is brown.

      Note: If the student's name ends with **s**, just add an apostrophe.
      Ex: Les' book (or Les's book)

   e. When there is more than one owner of something, we call it **plural possessive noun**.
      Ex: The computer is in the *girls'* room.
           The room belongs to more than one girl.

      Look at the first line in the poetry verse. What is the plural possessive noun?

   f. What do you notice about the apostrophe when the noun is plural and ends with an **s**?

2.
a. the boy

b. Freedom's

c. 1) keys   brother
    2) dish   dog
    3) nest   bird

d. Answers will vary.

e. fathers'

f. Just add an apostrophe (').

2.

g. For most plural nouns ending in s, just add an apostrophe (').

h. 1) Where are the teachers' cards?
2) Where are the kids' toys?
3) Where are the farmers' vegetables?
4) Where are the girls' shorts?
5) Where are the boys' gloves?

3.

b. a a b c c c b

c. Answers will vary.

g. Can you make up a rule that tells how to make plural nouns possessive?

h. Use a plural possessive noun to form sentences.
Ex: Where are the *bowls belonging to the dogs*?
Where are the *dogs' bowls*?

1) Where are the cars belonging to the teachers?
2) Where are the tows belonging to the kids?
3) Where are the vegetables belonging to the farmers?
4) Where are the shorts belonging to the girls?
5) Where are the gloves belonging to the boys?

3. a. A **rhyme** consists of two words in which the end sounds of the words are alike. In poetry, two lines are said to rhyme if the words at the ends of the lines rhyme. Look at the first verse of "America," by Samuel Francis Smith found in Lesson 1. Look at the end word of line one and mark it **a**. Look for all the end words that rhyme with *thee*, and mark them with an **a**. Look at the end word of line three and mark it **b**. Now, mark the end word of line four with **c**. Find the end words that rhyme with *died* and mark them with **c**. This is called the **rhyme scheme** of the poem. In this case, the rhyme scheme is – a a b c c c b.

b. Now use the same process to mark the lines in verse four of "America," found in this lesson. What is the rhyme scheme of verse four?

c. Write a series of words with the same rhyme scheme as in "America."
Ex: best, rest; day; night, light; sight; play

d. If you would like, try to write a poem with the same rhyme scheme and meter as used in "America." You may use your rhyming words from **3c**.

Ex: My poodle is the *best*.
     At getting lots of *rest*.
     He sleeps all *day*.
     When I lie down at *night*.
     My dog turns on the *light*.
     He keeps me in his *sight*.
     He wants to *play*.

e. Review your spelling words.

4. a. Reread the excerpt on page 15 of the book *Patriotic Songs* regarding the song "America." Read the excerpt silently or aloud to your teacher.

   b. This poem reflects Samuel's love of our patriotic history. As a young boy, he was very interested in the ride of Paul Revere. Read about Paul Revere in an encyclopedia or history book and write one or two sentences telling why this ride was such an important part of our history.

4.

b. Paul Revere's ride was important because it warned the people of the English invasion.

   c. Why do you think Samuel thought it was so exciting?

c. Answers may vary.

   d. Read "Paul Revere's Ride" by Henry Wadsworth Longfellow and color in the illustration of Samuel thinking about the ride of Paul Revere on page 29.

Paul Revere's Ride
Henry Wadsworth Longfellow

Listen, my children, and you shall hear
Of the midnight ride of Paul Revere,
On the eighteenth of April, in Seventy-five;
Hardly a man is now alive
Who remembers that famous day and year.

He said to his friend, "If the British mark
By land or sea from the town to-night
Hang a lantern aloft in the belfry arch
Of the North Church tower as a signal light,—

One, if by land, and two, if by sea;
And I on the opposite shore will be,
Ready to ride and spread the alarm

Through every Middlesex village and farm,
For the country folk to be up and to arm."

Then he said, "Good night!" and with muffled oar
Silently rowed to the Charleston shore,
Just as the moon rose over the bay,
Where swinging wide at her moorings lay
The *Somerset*, British man-of-war;
A phantom ship, with each mast and spar
Across the moon like a prison bar,
And a huge black hulk, that was magnified
By its own reflection in the tide.

Meanwhile, his friend, through alley and street,
Wanders and watched with eager ears,
Till in the silence around him he hears
The muster of men at the barrack door,
The sound of arms, and the tramp of feet,
And the measured tread of the grenadiers,
Marching down to their boats on the shore.

Then he climbed the tower of the Old North Church,
By the wooden stairs, with stealthy tread,
To the belfry-chamber overhead,
And startled the pigeons from their perch
On the somber rafters, that round him made
Masses and moving shapes of shade, —
By the trembling ladder, steep and tall,
To the highest window in the wall,
Where he paused to listen and look down
A moment on the roofs of the town,
And the moonlight flowing over all.

Beneath, in the churchyard, lay the dead,
In their night-encampment on the hill,
Wrapped in silence so deep and still
That he could hear, like a sentinel's tread,
The watchful night-wind, as it went
Creeping along from tent to tent,
And seeming to whisper, "All is well!"
A moment only he feels the spell
Of the place and the hour, and the secret dread
Of the lonely belfry and the dead;
For suddenly all his thoughts are bent
On a shadowy something far away,
Where the river widens to meet the bay, —
A line of black that bends and floats

On the rising tide, like a bridge of boats.

Meanwhile, impatient to mount and ride,
Booted and spurred, with a heavy stride
On the opposite shore walked Paul Revere.
Now he patted his horse's side,
Now gazed at the landscape far and near,
Then, impetuous, stamped the earth,
And turned and tightened his saddle-girth;
But mostly he watched with eager search
The belfry-tower of the Old North Church,
As it rose above the graves on the hill,
Lonely and spectral and somber and still.

And lo! As he looks, on the belfry's height
A glimmer, and then a gleam of light!
He springs to the saddle, the bridle he turns,
But lingers and gazes, till full on his sight
A second lamp in the belfry burns!

A hurry of hoofs in a village street,
A shape in the moonlight, a bulk in the dark,
And beneath, from the pebbles, in passing, a spark
Stuck out by a steed flying fearless and fleet;
That was all! And yet, through the gloom and the light
The fate of a nation was riding that night;
And the spark struck out by that steed in his flight,
Kindled the land into flame with its heat.

He has left the village and mounted the steep,
And beneath him, tranquil and broad and deep,
Is the Mystic, meeting the ocean tides;
And under the alders, that skirt its edge,
Now soft on the sand, now loud on the ledge,
Is heard the tramp of his steed as he rides.

It was twelve by the village clock
When he crossed the bridge into Medford town.
He heard the crowing of the cock,
And the barking of the farmer's dog,
And felt the damp of the river fog,
That rises after the sun goes down.

It was one by the village clock,
When he galloped into Lexington.
He saw the gilded weathercrock
Swim in the moonlight as he passed,

And the meeting-house windows, blank and bare,
Gaze at him with a spectral glare,
As if they already stood aghast
At the bloody work they would look upon.

It was two by the village clock,
When he came to the bridge in Concord town.
He heard the bleating of the flock,
And the twitter of birds among the trees,
And felt the breath of the morning breeze
Blowing over the meadows brown.
And one was safe and asleep in his bed
Who at the bridge would be first to fall,
Who that day would be lying dead,
Pierced by a British musket-ball.

You know the rest. In the books you have read,
How the British Regulars fired and fled, —
How the farmers gave them ball for ball,
From behind each fence and farmyard wall,
Chasing the redcoats down the lane,
Then crossing the fields to emerge again
Under the trees at the turn of the road,
And only pausing to fire and load.
So through the night rode Paul Revere;
And so through the night went his cry of alarm
To every Middlesex village and farm, —
A cry of defiance, and not of fear,
A voice in the darkness, a knock at the door,
And a word that shall echo forevermore!
For, borne on the night-wind of the Past,
Through all our history, to the last,
In the hour of darkness and peril and need,
The people will waken and listen to hear
The hurrying hoofbeats of that steed,
And the midnight message of Paul Revere.

e. Optional: Take an oral or written spelling pretest.

Used by permission from *Color the Patriotic Classics*. One in the series of historical books and musical cassette tapes from *Color the Classics* by Carmen Ziarkowski.

5.

a. Answers will vary.

5. a. We have spent two weeks studying verses from Samuel Francis Smith's poem "America." Using the memorization tips outline in Lesson 1 on page 16, memorize the last verse of the poem. When you have learned this verse, combine it with the verse you memorized last week, and present the poem (either by speaking or singing) to your family or class. You may memorize the poem you wrote this week and present it also.

America
by Samuel Francis Smith

My country, 'tis of thee,
Sweet land of liberty,
   Of thee I sing;
Land where my fathers died,
Land of the Pilgrims' pride,
From every mountainside
   Let Freedom ring.

My native country, thee,
Land of the noble free—
   Thy name I love;
I love thy rocks and rills,
Thy woods and templed hills;
My heart and rapture thrills
   Like that above.

Let music swell the breeze,
And ring form all the trees,
   Sweet freedom's song;
Let mortal tongues awake,
Let all that breathe partake,
Let rocks their silence break—
   The sound prolong.

Our fathers' God, to Thee,
Author of liberty,
   To Thee we sing;
Long may our land be bright
With Freedom's holy light;
Protect us by Thy might,
   Great God, our King!

We often only learn one or two verses of a poem or song, missing the beautiful and meaningful language of the other verses. Read silently or listen to your teacher read the entire song. What meaning did the other verses add to your understanding of Smith's poem "America?"

You may want to try to memorize and present all four verses of this poem to your family or class.

b. Take a spelling test.

c. Optional: Choose skills from the *Review Activities* on the next page.

Review Activities

Choose the skills your student needs to review.

1. *Homonyms*
   Complete the sentences with the correct word.

   a. My brother was an (hour, our) late.
   b. We hope you enjoy (hour, our) play.
   c. Julie has (to, two, too) cats.
   d. She gave one (to, two, too) me.
   e. Now, Steven wants a cat (to, two, too).

2. *Singular Possessive Nouns*
   Change the following to its possessive form.

   a. the costume of the boy
   b. the blanket of the baby
   c. the voice of the singer
   d. the house of the neighbor

3. *Plural Possessive Nouns*
   Change the following to its possessive form.

   a. the costumes of the boys
   b. the blankets of the babies
   c. the voices of the singers
   d. the houses of the neighbors

4. Name two rhyming words for the following:

   a. went
   b. beat
   c. drink
   d. seem
   e. all

5. *Poetry Memorization*
   Recite verse four of "America."

1.
a. hour
b. our
c. two
d. to
e. too

2.
a. boy's costume
b. baby's blanket
c. singer's voice
d. neighbor's house

3.
a. boys' costumes
b. babies' blankets
c. singers' voices
d. neighbors' houses

4. Possible answers:
a. sent, bent, cent, lent, meant, rent, etc.
b. heat, seat, treat, meat, cheat, wheat, etc.
c. sink, mink, link, blink, shrink, pink, etc.
d. team, beam, dream, steam, cream, etc.
e. tall, ball, fall, mall, call, doll, wall, etc.

EVERYDAY WORDS

in
Mr. Popper's Penguins

Skills

Adjective	Paragraph
Addressing an Envelope	Plurals
Adverb	Sentence
Base or root word	Subject and predicate
Capitalization	Suffix
Comma	Synonym
Comma and proper noun	Verb
Double negative	Writing a card
Hyphen	

Teacher's Note: As your student completes each lesson, choose skills from the Review Activities that he needs. The Review Activities follow each lesson.

Next day the picture of Mr. Popper and Captain Cook appeared in the Stillwater Morning Chronicle, with a paragraph about the house painter who had received a penguin by air express from Admiral Drake in the faraway Antartica. *Then the Associated Press picked up the story, and a week later the photograph, in rotogravure, could be seen in the Sunday edition of the most important newspapers in all the largest cities in the country.*

1. a. Read the literature passage silently. Ask your teacher to help you with difficult words. When you are ready, read the passage out loud to your teacher. In your own words, tell your teacher what is happening in this passage. This is called **narration**.

    b. As your teacher reads the lines in bold print out loud, write them down. Compare your copy to the literature passage and make corrections.

    c. List four to six words that you should study for spelling this week, or use the following list of suggested words: picture, appeared, received, paragraph.

    Words with the sound **/cher/** are sometimes spelled **-ture**.

> ### Spelling Tip
> The **/cher/** sound in words like *nature* is sometimes spelled **-ture**.

Copy these words and underline **-ture**. Read the words aloud as your write them.

picture	mature
nature	feature
pasture	rapture
miniature	vulture

2. a. A **complete sentence** is a complete thought. It tells who or what the sentence is about. It also tells something about the thing or person.

   Ex: *Lives in a nice, little house* – This is an incomplete sentence. It does not tell who or what. This is called a **fragment**.
   Jamie and Bill – This is an incomplete sentence. It does not tell something about Jamie and Bill. This is also a fragment.
   Jamie and Bill lived in a nice little house. This is a complete sentence.

   b. Read the following sentences and write **F** (Fragment) or **C** (Complete sentence).

      1) The penguins rode the bus.
      2) The people of Stillwater.
      3) Is a house painter.
      4) Wanted to be a scientist.
      5) The penguins waved good-bye.

   c. A sentence contains two parts: the complete subject and the complete predicate. The **complete subject** tells who or what the sentence is about. The **complete predicate** tells something about the subject.

      Draw a vertical line to separate the complete subject and the complete predicate.
      Ex: The Poppers / felt very proud and happy.

      1) Captain Cook ate all the goldfish.
      2) A policeman visited the Popper's home.
      3) The penguins did not like the heat.
      4) Greta laid the eggs.
      5) Captain Cook and Greta loved the ice.

2.
b. 1) C
   2) F
   3) F
   4) F
   5) C

c. 1) Captain Cook / ate all the goldfish
   2) A policemen / visited the Popper's home.
   3) The penguins / did not like the heat.
   4) Greta / laid the eggs.
   5) Captain Cook and Greta / loved the ice.

2.
d. Answers will vary.

3.
A. Next, Mr. Popper,
   Captain Cook,
   Stillwater Morning
   Chronicle, Admiral
   Drake, Then,
   Antarctica, Associated
   Press, Sunday

c. Possible Answers:
   1) Africa, Australia
   2) January
   3) Saturn, Pluto
   4) Sara, Jessica

d. Pretend an animal—any animal—is delivered to your home by mistake. The zoo keeper says he can't pick up the animals until tomorrow, so you'll have to care for it for one day. Luckily, the animal comes with a leash.

Discuss this situation with your teacher. You might wonder where you will keep the animal, or what to feed it. Will you be able to play with it? What if the neighbors see it?

After your discussion, write a paragraph of at least five sentences about the day a zoo animal was delivered to your house by mistake. A **paragraph** contains sentences about a main topic. **Indent** the first line of your paragraph by starting about half an inch from the left margin.

You may want to draw a picture that illustrates your story.

3. a. Look at the literature passage again. There are many words in the passage which start with a **capital letter**. Every time we see a capital letter, an imaginary bell should ring in our minds. That bell reminds us that we should think about why the word starts with a capital letter. The capital letter gives us information that will help us understand what we are reading. Using a colored pencil or a highlighter marker, underline or mark all the words of the literature passage that begin with a capital letter.

b. Nouns which begin with a lower case letter are called **common nouns**. Common nouns name any person, place, thing, or idea. When we speak about a particular person, place, thing, or idea, we use a capital letter. These words are called **proper nouns**.

Ex: **Common nouns**   **Proper nouns**
     boy   George
     city   Atlanta
     day   Saturday

c. Write proper nouns for the following common nouns. Remember to begin with a capital letter.

1) continent   2) month   3) planet   4) girl

d. Each of the words you highlighted or underlined is capitalized for a reason. Here are several reasons why words are capitalized.

Rule 1	Use a capital letter to begin a sentence

Rule 2	Use a capital letter to begin the names of holidays, months and days. (Ex: New Year's Day)

Rule 3	Use a capital letter when writing the names of places, such as streets, towns, or countries. (Ex: Oak Street)

Rule 4	Use a capital letter to begin the name of a business or organization (Ex: Boys Scouts of America)

Rule 5	Use a capital letter to begin the name of a person or pet. Each word in a person's name is capitalized. (Ex: Robert J. Owens)

Rule 6	Use a capital letter to begin the first word and each important word in titles of books, newspapers, movies, works of art or other titles. (Ex: *Old Yeller*)

Rule 7	Use a capital letter to begin a title of a person, or the abbreviation of the title. (Ex: Dr. Money)

Write the capitalization rules on index cards, or cut them out of your *Student Activity Book* page 37.

Note: Keep these cards available. You will need them in future lessons.

e. Match the capitalized words that you highlighted in the literature passage in **3a** to the corresponding rules. Write the words on the back of the correct cards. This gives you at least one example for each rule. Keep these cards. We will use them again later, and add more capitalization rules.

f. Below the literature passage is the title of the book. Why is the apostrophe used in *Mr. Popper's*?

3.
e. Next, Then – Rule 1
Mr., Captain, Admiral – Rule 7
Popper, Cook, Drake – Rule 5
Stillwater Morning Chronicle – Rule 6
Associated Press – Rule 4 or 6
Antarctica – Rule 3
Sunday – Rule 2

f. The penguins belong to Mr. Popper

g. Capitalization Rule 6 tells us to capitalize the first word and every other important word in the titles of books. Also, remember to underline the title. If you are using a computer use italics instead.

Imagine if the author wrote books about other people with strange animals for pets. Write the possessive nouns as the title using this example as a guideline.
Ex: the penguins belonging to Mr. Popper
   Mr. Popper's Penguins or *Mr. Popper's Penguins*

1) the flamingo belonging to Fanny
2) the ostrich belonging to Oscar
3) the llama belonging to Larry
4) the manatee belonging to Maria
5) the aardvark belonging to Arnie

h. Review your spelling words.

4. a. You learned about complete sentences in **2a**. Read the following sentences.
   1) I like to eat ice cream.
   2) Do you like to eat ice cream?
   3) Wow, I really like ice cream!
   4) Come get your ice cream.

The first sentence makes a statement. This is called a **declarative sentence**. It ends with a period. (**.**)

The second sentence asks a question. This is called an **interrogative sentence**. It ends with a question mark. (**?**)

The third sentence has strong or sudden feeling. This is called an **exclamatory sentence**. It ends with an exclamation mark. (**!**).

The fourth sentence makes a request or a command. This is called an **imperative sentence**. It can end with a period (**.**) or exclamation mark (**!**).

Write a declarative, interrogative, exclamatory, and imperative sentence. Use the correct punctuation.

3.
g. 1) <u>**Fanny's Flamingo**</u> **or**
Fanny's Flamingo
2) <u>**Oscar's Ostrich**</u> **or**
Oscar's Ostrich
3) <u>**Larry's Llama**</u> **or**
Larry's Llama
4) <u>**Maria's Manatee**</u> **or**
Maria's Manatee
5) <u>**Arnie's Aardvark**</u> **or**
Arnie's Aardvark

4.
a. **Answers will vary.**

b. In the literature passage, there are two words that mean about the same thing. Find the word *photograph* in the literature passage and write it down. There is another word in the passage that has about the same meaning. Find it and write it beside the word *photograph*. Words that are close in meaning are called **synonyms**.

c. A **thesaurus** is a book of synonyms. If you need help, use a thesaurus to look up synonyms for the following words taken from the literature passage.
   1) faraway
   2) later
   3) large

d. Read the sentences from which the above words were taken. Replace the words with the synonyms you chose. How do the sentences sound to you now?

e. Is the meaning the same? When you are having trouble thinking of the right word to use when you are writing, thesaurus will be a big help.

f. Optional: Take an oral or written spelling pretest.

5. a. Listen as your teacher reads the first sentence of the literature passage. You will now write the passage from dictation. Do not write as it is read the first time. Just listen. Remember, writing from dictation is a skill you acquire with practice, like hitting a baseball. Your first attempts may not be too successful, but as you practice you will become better.

   b. After you listen to the literature passage the second time, write what you have heard. When you have finished, compare your copy to the literature passage.

   c. Optional: Take a spelling test.

   d. Optional: Choose skills from the *Review Activities* on the next page.

4.
b. photograph – picture

4.
c. 1) distant
   2) after
   3) big

d. **Answers will vary.**

e. **Yes**

Review Activities

Choose the skills your student needs to review.

1. *Sentence / Fragment*
   Read the following sentences, and tell if they are a complete sentence (**C**) or a fragment (**F**).

   a. Smiled happily at her father.
   b. Brian fixed the flat tire.
   c. Tomorrow is Friday.
   d. Jacob and Travis.
   e. Sent a letter.
   f. I went home.

2. *Complete Subject / Predicate*
   Draw a vertical line between the complete subject and predicate.

   a. Russell saved his allowance.
   b. I take piano lessons.
   c. The dog walked with a limp.
   d. Jeremy hit a homerun.
   e. The coach praised his team.
   f. A big smile broke across his face.

3. *Common and Proper Nouns*
   Name a proper noun for each common noun.

   a. day of the week
   b. boy
   c. country
   d. city

1.
a. F
b. C
c. C
d. F
e. F
f. C

2.
a. Russell / saved his allowance
b. I / take piano lessons.
c. The dog / walked with a limp.
d. Jeremy / hit a homerun.
e. The coach / praised his team.
f. A big smile / broke across his face.

3. Possible Answers:
a. Monday, Tuesday, etc.
b. Russell, Steve, Benjamin, etc.
c. Canada, France, China, etc.
d. Chicago, Seattle, Denver, etc.

4. *Capitalization*
   Capitalize the following sentences, and add punctuation.

   a. my cousin lives in alabama
   b. the baby was born on saturday
   c. yesterday, cindy met mr. wilson
   d. robert joined the boy scouts
   e. we learned about jupiter and venus
   f. are you leaving on friday
   g. help me out of here
   h. have you read the prince and the pauper

5. *Titles of Books*
   Write the titles of the following books.

   a. the house of sixty fathers
   b. the secret garden
   c. the cabin faced west
   d. a bear called paddington

6. *Types of Sentences / Punctuation*
   Punctuate the following sentences and tell if they are
   declarative (**Dec**), interrogative (**Int**), exclamatory (**Exc**), or
   imperative (**Imp**).

   a. Justin is eleven years old
   b. How old is Sherry
   c. Please come here
   d. There's a snake outside

7. *Synonyms*
   Replace the italicized word with a synonym.

   a. Warren spoke *softly*.
   b. The man was *nice*.
   c. The boy *hit* the ball.
   d. I was *surprised*.

4.
a. **My cousin lives in Alabama.**
b. **The baby was born on Saturday.**
c. **Yesterday, Cindy met Mr. Wilson.**
d. **Robert joined the Boy Scouts.**
e. **We learned about Jupiter and Venus.**
f. **Are you leaving on Friday?**
g. **Help me out here!**
h. **Have you read The Prince and the Pauper?**

5.
a. **The House of Sixty Fathers** or *The House of Sixty Fathers*
b. **The Secret Garden** or *The Secret Garden*
c. **The Cabin Faced West** or *The Cabin Faced West*
d. **A Bear called Paddington** or *A Bear Called Paddington*

6.
a. **Justin is eleven years old. (Dec)**
b. **How old is Sherry? (Int)**
c. **Please come here. (Imp)**
d. **There's a snake outside! (Exc)**

7. **Possible answers:**
a. **quietly, gently**
b. **pleasant, kind, good**
c. **whacked, struck, slugged**
d. **astonished, amazed, startled, stunned**

✎ **Teacher's Note:** As
your student completes
each lesson, choose skills
from the Review Activities
that he needs. The
Review Activities follow
each lesson.

1.
**b. A breeding ground of
birds and animals.**

*Captain Cook was not happy,
however. He had suddenly ceased his
gay, exploring little walks about the house
and would sit most of the day, sulking, in
the refrigerator.* Mr. Popper had removed
all the stranger objects, leaving only the
marbles and checkers, so that Captain
Cook now had a nice, orderly little rookery.
    "Better leave him alone, children," said
Mrs. Popper. "He feels mopy, I guess."

From **Mr. Popper's Penguins** by Richard and Florence Artwater. Copyright
©1938 by Florence Atwater and Richard Artwater.
© Renewed 1966 by Florence Artwater, Doris Artwater, and Carroll
Artwater Bishop. By permission of Little, Broward and Company.

1. a. Read the literature passage silently. Ask your teacher to
    help you with difficult words. When you are ready, read
    the passage out loud to your teacher.

   b. Find the word *rook* in a dictionary, in which the definition
    refers to a bird. Glancing down, find the word *rookery*.
    Rookery has several definitions. What does the word
    rookery mean in our story?

   c. As your teacher reads the lines in bold print out loud,
    write them down. Compare your copy to the literature
    passage and make corrections.

   d. List four to six words that you and your teacher
    decide you should study this week for spelling, or
    use the following list of suggested words: exploring,
    refrigerator, suddenly, ceased.

   A **suffix** is a letter or group of letters added to the end of a
   base or **root word**. The suffix often changes the part of the
   speech or tense. (You will learn more about this in Day 3)

   Before you add the suffix **-ed** or **-ing** to a word, look at
   the word. If the words ends with a silent **e**, drop the **e**
   before adding **-ed** or **-ing**.

Spelling Tip
Drop the silent **e** before adding a
suffix beginning with a vowel.

e. Add the suffix **-ed** and **-ing** to the following words.

	-ed	**-ing**
Ex: cease	ceased	ceasing

   1) explore
   2) bake
   3) hope
   4) joke
   5) name
   6) hire

2. a. You have learned that a sentence contains a complete subject and a predicate. Look at the following sentence and divide the complete subject and predicate with a vertical line:

     The happy children played at the park.

b. What is the main word in the predicate which shows action without any describing words? Underline that word. The word *played* is a **verb**. A verb can show action such as *run, laugh, sleep*, etc. These are called **action verbs**.

A verb can show action, but it can also be any form of the word *be*. These words are called **being verbs**.

Being Verbs
am   is   are   was
were   being   been

c. Using the following sentences, draw a vertical line between the complete subject and the predicate. Underline the verb twice, and tell whether it is an action (**A**) or being verb (**B**).

   1) Mr. Popper moved the furniture.
   2) The children played on the ice.
   3) Greta was happy and healthy.
   4) The penguins were happier in the cold.
   5) The warm weather melted the ice.

3. a. Sometimes a verb will have another verb helping it. These words are called **helping verbs**.

1.
e. 1) explored   exploring
   2) baked   baking
   3) hoped   hoping
   4) joked   joking
   5) named   naming
   6) hired   hiring

2.
a. The happy children / played at the park.

b. played

c. 1) Mr. Popper / <u>moved</u> the furniture. (A)
2) The children / <u>played</u> on the ice. (A)
3) Greta / <u>was</u> happy and healthy. (8)
4) The penguins / <u>were</u> happier in the cold. (13)
5) The warm weather / <u>melted</u> the ice. (A)

Helping Verbs			
have	has	had	do
does	did	shall	will
would	could	should	may
must	can		

Being verbs can also be helping verbs.

Look at this simplified sentence from the literature passage: He had suddenly ceased his gay, little walks.

A verb with a helping verb is called a **verb phrase**. A verb phrase may have more than one helping verb. Sometimes a verb phrase may be broken up with another word, as in the sentence above. *Had ceased* is the verb phrase.

b. Read the following sentences. Underline the verb phrase twice and circle the helping verbs.
   1) The bus had gone downtown.
   2) Boxes were brought aboard the ship.
   3) Mr. Popper was wiping the tears from his eyes.
   4) He had been sleeping for a long time.
   5) Columbus had sparred with Nelson.

c. Write the words from the literature passage that end with the suffix **-ing**.

d. When we add **-ing** to the end of the word we have added a suffix. Think about this picture. The base word, or word without anything added to it, is like the main house. A suffix is a letter or letters that is added to the end of the word, like an extra room on a house. The extra room adds more uses to the house. The suffix that is put on the end of the word adds another way the word can be used.

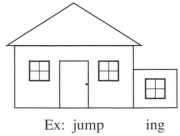

Ex: jump   ing

Beside each **-ing** word you wrote in, write the base word.

Answer column (left margin)

3.
b. 1) The bus (had) gone downtown.
   2) Boxes (were) brought aboard the ship.
   3) Mr. Popper (was) wiping the tears from his eyes.
   4) He (had) (been) sleeping for a long time.
   5) Columbus (had) sparred with Nelson.

c. exploring
   sulking
   leaving

d. exploring-explore
   sulking-sulk
   leaving-leave

e. To show that something is continuing to happen, we add the suffix **-ing**. There are three ways to add **-ing** to a word. Cut them out and glue each of them on an index cards; or you may cut them out from your *Student Activity Book* on page 49. Listen as your teacher reads them to you.

---

1. When you add a suffix to a word ending in silent **e**, drop the **e** before adding an ending that begins with a vowel.
    Ex: make / making

2. When you add a suffix to a word ending with a short vowel and a consonant, double the final consonant before adding an ending beginning with a vowel.
    Ex: hop / hopping

3. When you add a suffix to a word that has a long vowel before a consonant, or to a word with a short vowel before two consonants, just add the ending.
    Ex: mow / mowing   bend / bending

Match the words below to the correct rule. Write the correct word on the back of each card.
     sulk   swim   leave

f. Look at these words. Remember the rules above and add **-ing**. Which of the three rules would apply?
     spend   take   sit
     explore   clap   play

g. Review your spelling words

4. a. **Adjectives** are words that tell something about nouns and pronouns. Adjectives describe nouns and pronouns by telling what kind, whose, which one, or how many.

   The word *rookery* is described in our episode. Write the words that describe *rookery*.

   These words are adjectives because they tell about Captain Cook's rookery.

3.
e. sulk - sulking
   Rule 3
   swim - swimming
   Rule 2
   leave - leaving
   Rule 1

f. spend- spending Rule 3
   take - taking   Rule 1
   sit a sitting   Rule 2
   explore -exploring Rule 1
   clap - clapping   Rule 2
   play - playing   Rule 3

4.
a. nice, orderly, little

4.

b. Answers will vary.

c. Answers will vary.
The following may be
helpful.
- **water bird**
- **warmblooded**
- **Antarctica**
- **lays eggs**
- **can grow to 3ft. tall etc.**

d. Answers will vary.

b. Think of words you can use to describe penguins. Draw a picture.

c. In our literature passage, Captain Cook is a penguin. Using an encyclopedia or a book about penguins, make a list of at least five **facts** (a true statement) about them. A list does not have to be in complete sentences. Include basic information, such as where they live (habitat), and how they produce offspring.

d. Imagine you have a pet penguin and he is walking around your living room while you watch him. Compose a paragraph of several sentences describing what your penguin does and how he looks as he walks around. Begin your paragraph by indenting about half an inch from the left margin. Use the words you listed in **4b** and the information you listed in **4c**. Try to use adjectives in your writing.

e. Optional: Take an oral or written spelling pretest.

5. a. Listen as your teacher reads the literature passage for dictation. Do not write as it is read the first time. Just listen. Remember, writing from dictation is a skill you acquire with practice, like hitting a baseball. Your first attempts may not be too successful, but as you practice you will become better.

b. After you listen to the literature passage the second time, write what you have heard. When you have finished, compare your copy to the literature passage.

c. Optional: Take a spelling test.

d. Optional: Choose skills from the *Review Activities* on the next page.

Review Activities

Choose the skills your student needs to review.

1. *Action and Being Verb*
   Underline the verb and tell if it is an action verb (**A**) or being verb (**B**).

   a. Dad runs three miles every day.
   b. Rachel drove to Atlanta.
   c. The boys are ten years old.
   d. I swept the floor.
   e. Becky is sick today.

2. *Helping Verb / Verb Phrase*
   Underline verb phrase and circle helping verb.

   a. The baby has been crying for an hour.
   b. I will be going soon.
   c. The weather should be nice tomorrow.
   d. Ralph must have cleaned his room.
   e. We will be moving next year.

3. *Adjectives*
   Complete the sentences with adjectives.

   a. The _____ clown made the crowd laugh.
   b. A _____ storm swept through the city.
   c. The _____ boy was glad to see his family.
   d. My sister made a _____ dinner for us.
   e. The man walked down the _____ path.

4. *Base Words and Suffix -ing.*
   Add the suffix **-ing** to the following words.

   a. help   f. sing
   b. take   g. come
   c. wash   h. run
   d. mop   1. draw
   e. call   j. fit

1.
a. <u>runs</u>   A
b. <u>drove</u>   A
c. <u>are</u>   B
d. <u>swept</u>   A
c. <u>is</u>   B

2.
a. (has been) crying
b. (will be) going
c. (should) be
d. (must have) cleaned
e. (will be) moving

3. Possible answers:
a. funny, little, etc.
b. big, terrible, etc.
c. little, worried
d. delicious, tasty, etc.
e. dark, sunny, etc.

4.
a. helping
b. taking
c. washing
d. moping
e. calling
f. singing
g. coming
h. running
i. drawing
j. fitting

Assessment 1
(Lessons 1 - 4)

1. Use the following sentences to complete exercises 1 - 3.

   a. The dog wagged his tail.
   b. My brother jumped on his bed.

   1) Draw a vertical line between the complete subject and the complete predicate.
   2) Underline the nouns.
   3) Circle the pronouns.

2. Capitalize the following sentences and add punctuation.

   a. when is tom coming
   b. he said he is coming on friday
   c. oh, here he is now

3. Write the possessive form for the following phrases.

   a. the dog belonging to my friend
   b. the computer belonging to Molly
   c. the coats belonging to the ladies

4. Underline the verbs in the following sentences. Tell if it is an action verb (**AV**) or a being verb (**BV**).

   a. There are five children at the park.
   b. The children flew their kites.
   c. After lunch, they played baseball.

5. The words *small* and *little* have the same or similar meaning. What are these kinds of words called?

6. The words *hole* and *whole* sound the same but have a different meaning and a different spelling. What are these kinds of words called?

7. Write three words which rhyme with *ate*.

1.
a. The <u>dog</u> / wagged (his) <u>tail</u>.
b. (My) <u>brother</u> / jumped on (his) <u>bed</u>.

2.
a. When is Tom coming?
b. He said he is coming on Friday.
c. Oh, here he is now. or Oh, here he is now!

3.
a. my friend's dog
b. Molly's computer
c. the ladies' coats

4.
a. There <u>are</u> five children at the park. - BV
b. The children <u>flew</u> their kites. - AV
c. After lunch, they <u>played</u> baseball. - AV

5. synonyms

6. Homonyms

7. Possible answers: mate, late, fate, rate, date, etc.

**But it was soon clear that it was
something worse than mopiness that
ailed Captain Cook. All day he would sit
with his little white-circled eyes staring
out sadly from the refrigerator.** *His coat
had lost its lovely, glossy look; his round,
little stomach grew flatter each day. He
would turn away now when Mrs. Popper
would offer him some canned shrimps.*

From *Mr. Popper's Penguins* by Richard and Florence Atwater.
Copyright ©1938 by Florence Atwater and Richard Atwater.
© Renewed 1966 by Florence Atwater, Doris Atwater, and Carroll Atwater Bishop.
By permission of Little, Brown and Company.

Teacher's Note: As
your student completes
each lesson, choose skills
from the Review Activities
that he needs. The
Review Activities follow
each lesson.

1. a. Read the literature passage silently. Ask your teacher to help you with difficult words. When you are ready, read the passage out loud to your teacher.

   b. As your teacher reads the lines in bold print out loud, write them down. Compare your copy to the literature passage and make corrections.

   c. List four to six words that you and your teacher decide you should study for spelling this week, or use the following list of suggested words: worse, mopiness, staring, refrigerator.

   Words with an **/er/** sound, preceded by **w** are usually spelled **wor**.

   ### Spelling Tip
   Words beginning with **w** followed by
   an **/er/** sound are spelled **wor**.

   d. Copy the following words and underline **wor**. Say the words aloud as you write them.

worse	worm
worth	word
world	worst
work	worry

2.

a. The happy <u>children</u> / played at the park.

b. 1) The <u>Popper's</u> / watched the penguins play.
   2) The funny <u>seals</u> / played with the penguins.
   3) Mr. Popper's <u>penguins</u> / became famous.
   4) Eight <u>suitcases</u> / were on the floor.
   5) The excited <u>director</u> / raised the curtain.

✐ **Teacher's Note:** If information on Captain Cook is unavailable, you may give your student the following information and ask him to make the timeline accordingly. This lesson teaches your student how to transfer information onto a chart, as well as prepare him in research skills.

c. 1728 - James Cook was born in England
1768 - 1st voyage to the Pacific Ocean
1770 - Discovered Botany Bay, Australia
1771 - Returned from first voyage
1772 - 1775 - 2nd voyage
1776 - 3rd voyage to Pacific
1778 - Discovered Hawaii
1779 - Died

d. Answers will vary.

---

2. a. Look at the sentence you worked with in Lesson 4:
The happy children played at the park.

The main word in the complete subject without any describing words is called the simple subject. The simple subject will always be a noun or pronoun. Draw a line between the complete subject and predicate. Find the simple subject in the sentence above and underline it once.

b. Separate the complete subject and predicate with a vertical line. Underline the simple subject once.
1) The Poppers watched the penguins play.
2) The funny seals played with the penguins.
3) Mr. Popper's penguins became famous.
4) Eight suitcases were on the floor.
5) The excited director raised the curtain.

From henceforth the simple subject will simply be referred to as the subject.

c. There was an explorer named Captain James Cook. Look up Captain James Cook in the encyclopedia, or books about explorers.

Make a time line, beginning with Captain James Cook's date of birth and ending with his death. Mark each voyage on the time line with a line and the date. Make a list including the dates of his birth, his major voyages, and his death. The following is a sample time line of Christopher Columbus.

Christopher Columbus
1492

His birth	Discovery of America	His death

d. Why do you think Mr. Popper named the penguin Captain Cook?

e. It is a special honor to name someone after someone else. Some children are given the same name as a relative to show honor or love for that relative. Do you know anyone in your family who is named after a relative or friend? Who were they named after and why?

f. Sometimes, people are not named after a relative, but after a famous person outside the family. Many people, for example, have been named after presidents. What does this tell us about how they feel about that famous person? Do you know someone who has been named after a famous person? If you could pick someone to be named after, who would he or she be and why?

3. a. Look at the last sentence of the first paragraph in the literature passage. It tells how Captain Cook's coat used to look. What two words describe this?

   b. Do you remember what these describing words are called?

   c. Look at the same sentence again. It also tells about his *round, little stomach*. What punctuation mark do you see between *round* and *little*?

   Separate two or more adjectives with a **comma**.
   Ex: Captain Cook looked pale, sick, and sad.
          His tired, dark eyes did not sparkle.

   d. Underline the adjectives and add commas.
   1) Greta enjoyed the fresh cool breeze.
   2) The funny delightful seals entertained the audience.
   3) Mr. Popper loved his kind dear wife.
   4) He brought out some red yellow and blue paint.
   5) They played on the slippery cold ice.

   e. Look at the picture,

   Write a sentence describing the house using two or more adjectives. Don't forget the commas.

   f. Possessive pronouns like *his, her, their, your,* and *its* are also adjectives. They describe a noun by telling "whose." List all the personal pronouns you can find in the literature passage. Circle all the possessive pronouns. (You may refer to the Personal Pronoun Chart on page 14.)

2.
e. Answers will vary.

f. Answers will vary.

3.
a. lovely, glossy

b. adjectives

c. comma

d. 1) Greta enjoyed the <u>fresh</u>, <u>cool</u> breeze.
2) The <u>funny</u>, <u>delightful</u> seals entertained the audience.
3) Mr. Popper loved his <u>kind</u>, <u>dear</u> wife.
4) He brought out some <u>red</u>, <u>yellow</u>, and <u>blue</u> paint.
5) They played on the <u>slippery</u>, <u>cold</u> ice.

3.
f. it, it, he, his, His, its, his, He, him.

51

4.

a. Possible Answers:
phone call, greeting
card, flowers, etc.

4. a. Captain Cook is like a sick friend. Think about ways you might help a sick friend.

   A get well card is a good way to encourage a sick friend. Design a get well card for a friend or family member. If you do not know anyone who is sick, write a "thinking of you" card. On the front of your card, you may place a picture, poem, or Scripture verse. The best ideas will come as you think of the sick person's personal interests, like baseball or horses. Inside your card, include a greeting, a brief message, and a closing.
   Ex:

   > *Dear Bob,*
   >
   > *I am sorry that you are sick. I hope you get well soon so we can play together. I'm lonely when I don't see you for several days. Get well soon.*
   >
   > *Your friend,*
   > *Bill*

   b. Look at the sample envelope below. Address an envelope for your letter, stamp it, and mail it.

   > *Bill Duck*
   > *678 Flamingo Street*
   > *Salem, OR 44444*
   >
   >   stamp
   >
   >   *Bob White*
   >   *123 Friend Avenue*
   >   *Salem, OR 44444*

   c. Review the seven rules for capitalization from Lesson 3. We will now add another rule about parts of a letter. Look at the rules you put on the cards from Lesson 3.

   Copy the following new rule on an index card or cut it out of your *Student Activity Book*.

   > **Rule 8**   Use a capital letter to begin all the words in the greeting and the first word in the closing of a letter.

4. d. Here are all the capitalizations rules you have learned.
      Refer to this list when you are not sure whether to use
      capitalization.

Capitalization Rules

Rule 1   Use a capital letter to begin a sentence.
Rule 2   Use a capital letter to begin the names of holidays,
         months, and days. (Ex: New Year's Day)
Rule 3   Use a capital letter when writing the names of places,
         such as streets, towns, or countries. (Ex: Oak Street)
Rule 4   Use a capital letter to begin the name of a business
         or organization. (Ex: Boy Scouts of America)
Rule 5   Use a capital letter anytime to begin a person's
         or pet's name. Each word in a person's name is
         capitalized.
         (Ex: Robert J. Owens)
Rule 6   Use a capital letter to begin the first word and each
         important word in the titles of books, newspapers,
         movies, works of art or other titles. (Ex: *Old Yeller*)
Rule 7   Use a capital letter to begin a title of a person.
         (Ex: Dr. Money)
Rule 8   Use a capital letter to begin all the words in the
         greeting and the first word in the closing of a letter.

Reread your letter and make sure all the words are capitalized
that should be capitalized, such as cities, states, streets, etc.

e. Optional: Take an oral or written spelling pretest.

5. a. Listen as your teacher reads the literature passage for
      dictation. Do not write as it is read the first time, just listen.
      Remember, writing from dictation is a skill you acquire
      with practice, like hitting a baseball. You first may not be
      too successful, but as you practice you will become better.

   b. After you listen to the literature passage the second time,
      write what you have heard. When you have finished,
      compare your copy to the literature passage.

   c. Optional: Take a spelling test.

   d. Optional: Choose skills from the *Review Activities* on the
      next page.

Review Activities

Choose the skills your student needs to review.

1. *Simple Subject*
   Draw a vertical line between the complete subject and predicate. Underline the simple subject once and underline the verb twice.

   a. A little bird perched on the window sill.
   b. It sang sweetly.
   c. Our family drove to Kentucky.
   d. Heavy rains fell last night.
   e. The annual fireworks were splendid.

2. *Adjectives and Commas*
   Underline the adjectives and add commas.

   a. Jessica watched the funny little monkeys.
   b. I swam in the cool clear water.
   c. Long dark shadows covered the ground.
   d. Pink white and purple flowers bordered the garden.
   e. We ate a healthy delicious meal.

3. *Possessive Pronouns*
   Are possessive pronouns (his, her, its, their, your) adjectives? Why?

4. *Letters*,
   Correct the following letter. Check for punctuation and capitalization.

   > *dear sam*
   >
   > *this week I have learned about letter writing. now that I know how to write a letter, you will hear from me more often.*
   >
   > *your pal*
   >
   > *casey*

1.
a. A little <u>bird</u> / <u>perched</u> on the window sill.
b. <u>It</u> / <u>sang</u> sweetly.
c. Our <u>family</u> / <u>drove</u> to Kentuky.
d. Heavy <u>rains</u> / <u>fell</u> last night.
e. The annual <u>fireworks</u> / <u>were</u> splendid.

2.
a. Jessica watched the <u>funny</u>, <u>little</u> monkeys.
b. I swam in the <u>cool</u>, <u>clear</u> water.
c. <u>Long, dark</u> shadows covered the ground.
d. <u>Pink</u>, <u>white</u> and <u>purple</u> flowers bordered the garden.
e. We ate a <u>healthy</u>, <u>delicious</u> meal.

3. Yes, because they answer the question "whose?"

4.

> *Dear Sam*
>
> *This week I have learned about letter writing. Now that I know how to write a letter, you will hear from me more often.*
> *Your pal,*
> *Casey*

That night the Poppers sat up all night, taking turns changing the ice packs.

It was no use. In the morning Mrs. Popper took Captain Cook's temperature again. It had gone up to one hundred and five.

Everyone was very sympathetic. The reporter on the Morning Chronicle *stopped to inquire about the penguin. The neighbors brought in all sorts of broths and jellies to try to temp the little fellow. Even Mrs. Callahan, who had never had a very high opinion of Captain Cook, made a lovely frozen custard for him. Nothing did any good. Captain Cook was too far gone.*

From ***Mr. Popper's Penguins*** by Richard and Florence Atwater. Copyright ©1938 by Florence Atwater and Richard Atwater. ©Renewed 1966 by Florence Atwater, Doris Atwater, and Carroll Atwater Bishop. By permission of Little, Brown and Company.

1. a. Read the literature passage silently. Ask your teacher to help you with difficult words. When you are ready, read the passage out loud to your teacher.

    b. As your teacher reads the lines in bold print out loud, write them down. Compare your copy to the literature passage and make corrections.

    c. List four to six words that you and your teacher decide you should study this week for spelling, or use the following list of suggested words: taking, changing, temperature, packs.

    When spelling a word that ends with a **/k/** sound, say the word aloud. If you hear a single short vowel before the **/k/** sound, it will often be spelled **ck**. If you hear a consonant sound after the short vowel, it will usually be spelled with just **k**.

> ### Spelling Tip
> A word with a short vowel sound followed by a **/k/** sound is often spelled **ck**.

d. Copy these words and underline **ck** and **k**. Say the words aloud as you write them.

ck	**k**
pack	plank
sick	stink
deck	elk
duck	dunk
sock	silk

2. a. Verbs can show "when" something is being done. This is called **verb tense**.

   Ex: Today, they walk.
   (This is happening now - present tense)
   Yesterday, they walked.
   (This happened yesterday - past tense)

   b. Most verbs change their tense in the following way. Look at the following **regular verbs**, and complete the chart with past tense verbs.

	Present Tense	**Past Tense**
Ex:	help	helped
1)	paint	
2)	wash	
3)	change	
4)	stop	
5)	inquire	
6)	tempt	

   Note: In the literature passage, some of the verbs used in the charts are verbals. This will be taught in a higher level *Learning Language Arts Through Literature*.

   c. Some verbs change completely when changing tense. These are called **irregular** verbs. Look at the following irregular verbs, and complete the chart with past tense verbs.

2.
b. PastTense
   1) painted
   2) washed
   3) changed
   4) stopped
   5) inquired
   6) tempted

	Present Tense	**Past Tense**
Ex:	grow	grew

1) fly
2) ring
3) sit
4) take
5) bring
6) make
7) do

d. When the situation worsened for Captain Cook, the literature passage for this lesson says that, "Everyone was sympathetic." What do you think the word *sympathetic* means? Don't look it up, but decide what you think it means by reading the rest of the passage. Tell your teacher your definition. You have used **context clues** to help you understand the meaning of the word.

3. a. Look at the first sentence of the literature passage. The word *ice packs* means more than one ice pack. This is called a **plural** noun. One ice pack is a **singular** noun.

   b. To form the plural of most nouns, just add **s**.
      Ex: room - rooms

      Looking at the literature passage, list all the plural nouns ending with just **s**.

   c. To form the plural of words ending in **ch**, **sh**, **s**, **z**, and **x**, add **es**. Say the word *beach*. Now say the word *beaches*. Can you hear the extra syllable? That usually means you add **-es**. Write the plural form for the following words. Listen for the extra syllable.
      Ex: beach - beaches
      1) dish
      2) kiss
      3) buzz
      4) ax

   d. To form the plural of words ending in **y**, first look at the word. If the word ends with a vowel and **y**, just add **s**.
      Ex: monkey - monkeys

2.
c. Past Tense
   1) flew
   2) rang
   3) sat
   4) took
   5) brought
   6) made
   7) did

d. pity or compassion

3.
b. Poppers, turns, ice packs, neighbors, sorts and broths.

c. yes
   1) dishes
   2) kisses
   3) buzzes
   4) axes

3.
e. jellies

f. 1) penguins
    2) guys
    3) days
    4) foxes
    5) captains
    6) bullies
    7) lunches
    8) chairs
    9) churches
   10) turkeys
   11) spies
   12) boxes
   13) cities
   14) masses

g. Answers will vary.

If the word ends with a consonant and **y**, change the **y** to **i** and add **es**.
Ex: lady - ladies

e. Looking at the literature passage, find the plural noun ending with **ies**.

f. Change the following singular nouns into plural nouns using the rules above.

1)	penguin	8)	chair
2)	guy	9)	church
3)	day	10)	turkey
4)	fox	11)	spy
5)	captain	12)	box
6)	bully	13)	city
7)	lunch	14)	mass

g. We learned in the literature passage in Lesson 3 that there had been a **newspaper article** about Captain Cook's arrival. It seems that people were interested in how he was doing. We see that Captain Cook has many visitors, one of whom is a reporter from the local newspaper. Imagine you are a reporter from your newspaper, and your assignment is to write about Captain Cook. Imagine that you arrive at the same time as the neighbors, and Captain Cook is surrounded by everyone who is handing out food and talking to him. First, write a few sentences reporting the facts from the passage. Next, write a few sentences describing how Captain Cook must fell and what he might be thinking. How would you fell if you were sick and surrounded by people holding out things, but you didn't know what they were saying?

Check to make sure you have the answered the 5 "W" questions that are used in **reporting**: Who? What? When? Where? Why?

h. Review your spelling words.

4. a. Look at the following sentence taken from the literature passage:

   Ex: Nothing did any good. (This is the correct way to use the negative word, *nothing*. Do not make the mistake of using two negative words together.)

   Ex: Nothing did no good. (This is incorrect. This is called a **double negative.**)

Look at the following negative words:

nothing   no   never   not   n't
hardly   barely   scarcely   nobody

Usually, to correct a double negative, change the word *no* to *any*; or take out one of the negative words.
   Ex: Nobody gave nothing. (double negative)
          Nobody gave anything. (correct)

          I didn't go to no stores. (double negative)
          I didn't go to any stores. (correct)

  b. Correct the following double negatives.
     1) Nobody went nowhere.
     2) I couldn't hardly believe it
     3) They didn't never come.

  c. Look at the last sentence of the second paragraph of the literature passage. Write the number word, *one hundred and five*. **Number words** from twenty-one to ninety-nine have **hyphens**.
     Ex: one hundred eighty-nine   thirty-six

Place hyphens correctly in the following number words.
     1) forty eight   4) fifty nine
     2) two hundred thirty two   5) six thousand twenty nine
     3) seventy one

  d. Rear Admiral Richard E. Byrd was a great Antarctic explorer. Look him up in the encyclopedia or a book about explorers. Write a few sentences about Byrd and his explorations. You may use the following questions to help you. Use complete sentences.

Teacher's Note: n't represents "not" in contractions.

4.
b. 1) Nobody went anywhere.
   2) I could hardly believe it.
   3) They never came.

c. 1) forty-eight
   2) two hundred thirty-two
   3) seventy-one
   4) fifty-nine
   5) six thousand twenty-nine

Teacher's Note: Help your student in the research process as needed.

4.

**d. 1) Byrd established
a permanent base in
Antarctica.
2) Byrd's base was
called Little America.
3) He had a permanent
place from which to
make explorations
4) It was the largest
Antarctic expedition in
history, with the help of
the U.S. Navy.
5) Byrd explored
Antarctica for about 28
years.**

e.

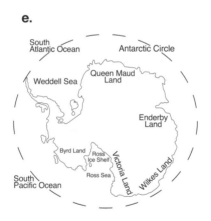

1) Tell me some things about Byrd's expeditions.
2) What was the name of Byrd's base in Antarctica?
3) What was the advantage of Byrd's permanent place?
4) What was special about Operation Highjump?
5) How many years (off and on) did Byrd explore Antarctica?

e. Using an **atlas** and pencil, fill in the following locations on your map of Antarctica, also found on page 69 of the *Student Activity Book*.

Atlantic Ocean	Pacific Ocean	Ross Sea
Antarctic Circle	Ross Ice	Weddell Sea

Label the continent with the following places.

Byrd Land	Victoria Land	Enderby Land
Wilkes Land	Queen Maud Land	

After checking your locations with your teacher, carefully trace over your pencil marks with a pen or fine tip marker. Locate Antarctica on a **globe** if available.

f. Take an oral or written spelling pretest.

5. a. Listen as your teacher reads the literature passage for dictation. Do not write as it is read the first time. Just listen. Remember, writing from dictation is a skill you acquire with practice, like hitting a baseball. Your first attempts may not be too successful, but as you practice you will become better at it.

   b. After you listen to the literature passage the second time, write what you have heard. When you have finished, compare your copy to the literature passage.

   c. Optional: Spelling test. After you write each word, use it in a sentence orally. When you are finished, compare your spelling to the correct spelling on your list, and make any needed corrections.

   d. Optional: Choose skills from the *Review Activities* on the next page.

Review Activities

Choose the skills your student needs to review.

1. *Verbe Tense*
   The following sentences are in the present tense. Rewrite them in the past tense.

   a. John washes the car.
   b. The children help mother.
   c. The bell rings loudly.
   d. The boy takes a big bite.
   e. Birds fly south for the winter.

2. *Plural Nouns*
   Write the plural form for the following words.

   a. church   b. tax
   c. donkey   d. box
   e. table   f. jelly
   g. bus   h. puppy

3. *Reporting*
   What are the five "W" questions used in reporting?

4. *Double Negatives*
   Correct the double negatives.

   a. Nobody never came.
   b. I can't hardly see.
   c. Nothing never goes right.

5. *Number words / Hyphens*
   Place hyphens in the following number words, if needed.

   a. twenty one
   b. four hundred
   c. seventy nine
   d. sixty two
   e. five thousand

1.
a. John washed the car.
b. The children helped mother.
c. The bell rang loudly.
d. The boy took a big bite.
e. Birds flew south for the winter.

2.
a. churches
b. taxes
c. donkeys
d. boxes
e. tables
f. jellies
g. buses
h. puppies

3. Who, what, when, where, why

4.
a. Nobody ever came.
b. I can hardly see.
c. Nothing ever goes right.

5.
a. twenty-one
b. four hundred
c. seventy-nine
d. sixty-two
e. five thousand

Surely if anyone anywhere had any idea what could cure a dying penguin, this man would.

Two days later there was an answer from the Curator. "Perhaps you do not know that we too have, in our aquarium at Mammoth City, a penguin from the Antarctic. It is failing rapidly, in spite of everything we have done for it. **I have wondered lately whether it is not suffering from loneliness. Perhaps that is what ails your Captain Cook. I am, therefore, shipping you, under separate cover, our penguin.** *You may keep her."*

And that is how Greta came to live at 432 Proudfoot Avenue.

1. a. Read the literature passage silently. Ask your teacher to help you with difficult words. When you are ready, read the passage out loud to your teacher.

   b. As your teacher reads the lines in bold print out loud, write them down. Did you remember to capitalize the entire name of Captain Cook? If you forgot, review Capitalization Rules on page 53. Compare your copy to the literature passage and make corrections.

   c. List four to six words that you should study for spelling this week, or use the following list of suggested words: wondered, loneliness, shipping, separate.

   Before you add a suffix beginning with a vowel, like -**ed** or **-ing** to a word, look at the word. If the word ends with a short vowel and one consonant, double the consonant before you add the suffix.

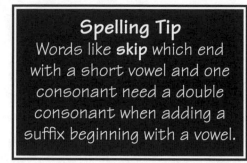

Spelling Tip
Words like **skip** which end with a short vowel and one consonant need a double consonant when adding a suffix beginning with a vowel.

d. Add the suffix. Say the words aloud as you read them.

	-ed	**-ing**
Ex: ship	shipped	shipping

1) stop
2) drag
3) fan
4) chop

1.
d. 1) stopped   stopping
   2) dragged   dragging
   3) fanned   fanning
   4) chopped   chopping

2. a. So far you have learned about four parts of speech: noun, verb, pronoun, and adjective. There are four more parts of speech; eight in all. You have learned that words which describe a person, place, thing, or idea are called adjectives.

Today, let's look at words which describe a verb. Look at the fourth sentence in the second paragraph of the literature passage. What word tells <u>when</u> *he wondered*? The word *lately* describes the verb, *wondered*. *Lately* is an adverb.

Adverbs can describe a verb by telling *when*, *where*, and *how*.
Ex: He wondered *lately*. - tells when
      He wondered as he sat *downstairs*. - tells where
      He wondered *intently*. - tells how

2.
b. **Possible answers:**
   1) Greta ran <u>slowly</u>.
   2) Greta ran <u>outside</u>.
   3) Greta ran <u>yesterday</u>.

b. Think of adverbs as you write the answers to the following sentences.
   1) Describe <u>how</u> Greta ran.
   2) Describe <u>where</u> Greta ran.
   3) Describe <u>when</u> Greta ran.

c. Adverbs can also describe adjectives. It can describe by telling *to what extent*.
   Ex: We have a *very* sick penguin. (*Sick* is an adjective, describing *penguin*. *Very* is an adverb, describing *sick*.)

d. Think of adverbs to complete these sentences.
   1) Mr. Popper was _____ happy.
   2) Captain Cook looks _____ funny.
   3) Mrs. Popper is a _____ nice woman.
   4) Jamie made a _____ nice home for the penguins.
   5) Bill was a _____ excited boy.

e. So far, we know that adverbs can describe a verb or an adjective. Lastly, adverbs can also describe other adverbs. Ex: It is failing *quite* rapidly. (*Quite* is an adverb, describing the adverb *rapidly*.)

Think of adverbs to complete these sentences.
1) Mrs. Popper spoke _____ firmly.
2) Mrs. Popper whistled _____ happily.
3) He turned _____ suddenly.

Hint

The word **not** and the contraction **n't** are adverbs.

---

f. Look at the five simple drawings on the next page, also found in the *Student Activity Book* on page 77. A picture represents each literature passage you have read in Lessons 3-7. (Remember, all the details of the story will not be in the picture, so look for the most important idea, or main idea, from each passage.) Put the five pictures in the correct order in which they happened in the story.

g. The literature passages we have read from *Mr. Popper's Penguins* are written as a narrative because they tell us the events of a story. When you tell the events of a story, you are **narrating**. Narrating is a good way to remember the events and details of a story.

h. After putting the pictures in order, retell the story of Captain Cook and the Poppers using your own words.

2.

d. Possible Answers:
1) very, so, really, extremely
2) very, so, really, incredibly
3) very, really, remarkably
4) very, really, surprisingly
5) very, really, overly

e. 1) unusually, quite
   2) extremely, very
   3) quite, very

f. Correct order:
1) **Front page of Morning Chronicle**
2) **Close-up of Captain Cook sulking**
3) **Captain Cook refusing the canned shrimp**
4) **Poppers, neighbors, and reporter, etc.**
5) **Crate at door from Mammoth City Aquarium**

h. Answers will vary.

Stillwater Morning Chronicle

Admiral Drake Sends Penguin To Mr. Popper

Early this morning, local resident, Mr. Popper, received an Air Express package containing a live penguin. The penguin, who Mr. Popper has affectionately named Captain Cook, was sent from Antarctica as a gift from Admiral Drake.

Neighbors of Mr. Popper are both curious and excited about the new addition to the town. "We'll all do our best to make the Captain feel at home!" exclaimed one neighbor.

Mr. Popper with his new pet, Captain Cook.

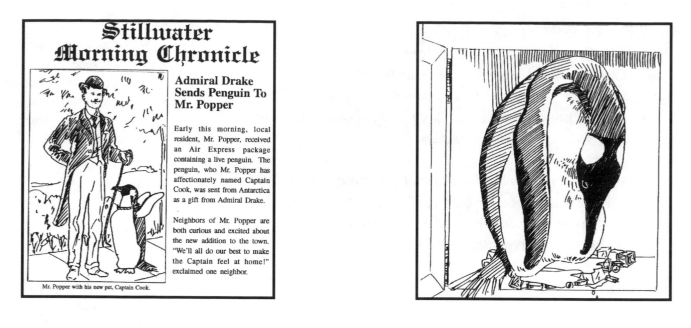

i. Using both the literature passages and the pictures, talk with your teacher and make up one sentence that tells the **main idea** or **topic** of each passage. Write it on the back of each picture.

3. a. In Lesson 6, you learned about making plurals. Before adding an **s** to words ending in **o**, look at the word. If the word ends with a vowel and **o**, just add **s**. If the word ends with a consonant and **o**, add **es**.

   Write the plural form for the following words.

	Singular	Plural
Ex:	rodeo	rodeos
	trio	
	studio	

	Singular	Plural
Ex:	tomato	tomatoes
	potato	
	echo	
	hero	

   b. All musical words ending in **o** form the plural by adding just **s**. Write the plural form for the following words.

	Singular	Plural
Ex:	banjo	banjos
	alto	
	piano	
	solo	

   c. Some nouns do not follow the rules. These words take on an irregular spelling.

   Look at the following words, and complete the chart. If you are not sure of the plural form, look in your dictionary.

	Singular	Plural
Ex:	child	children
	goose	
	foot	
	tooth	
	man	

3.
a. trios
studios

potatoes
echoes
heroes

b. altos
pianos
solos

c. geese
feet
teeth
men

✏ **Teacher's Note:** At this point, it might be confusing to introduce the subject of paragraph coherence. If your student relates the sentences in his paragraph to one topic, he will have achieved enough coherence for this age level.

d. Review your spelling words.

4. a. In Lessons 4-6, we have been accumulating information about Antarctica and explorers of Antarctica. We now have enough information to write a report.

A written **report** is organized so that your thoughts are in order. When your thoughts are in order they are easy to understand. The thoughts for your report are made into sentences. The sentences are made into paragraphs. Finally, the paragraphs are made into a report.

You have already written some sentences and a list in your research assignments during the past few weeks. Now it is time to make these sentences into paragraphs. A **paragraph** is a group of sentences about one main thing, called a **topic**. So far, your research has been Antarctica, penguins, Admiral Byrd, and Captain James Cook. When we write a paragraph, our first sentence tells the topic. The sentence is called the **topic sentence**. The rest of the sentences must tell us something about the topic.

For example, if your topic is penguins, you might have some sentences about penguins that look like this:

Penguins are birds.
They have wings, but they don't fly.
Penguins lay eggs in their nests.
Some different kinds of penguins are emperor, king, and macaroni.
Penguins live in the water, but they make nests on land.

We know that the topic for all our sentences is the penguin, but we need a topic sentence. A good topic sentence might be "Penguins are birds." **Indent** the first sentence of a paragraph by beginning about five spaces from the left margin. All the other sentences are about this topic. These are called **supporting sentences**. A good order, but not the only order for these sentences, might be like this:

> *Penguins are birds. They have wings, but they don't fly. Penguins live in the water, but they make nests on land. Penguins lay eggs in their nests. Some different kinds of penguins are emperor, king, and macaroni.*

Write a paragraph about Captain James Cook or Admiral Byrd. Include three to five sentences in your paragraph. Use the notes from the research which you did in previous lessons. You may use part of Day 5 to complete your writing.

b. Optional: Take an oral or written spelling pretest.

5. a. You have done a great deal of work gathering information and learning about Antarctic explorers. Now that you have finished writing a report, you should be very pleased with yourself. Share your report with your family or class by reading it to them and showing them any pictures you have drawn or the books you have used. You can also present your report to others by telling them what is in the report instead of reading it to them. It may seem hard to present reports orally at first. The more you practice, the easier it will become.

b. Optional: Take a spelling test.

c. Optional: Choose skills from the *Review Activities* on the next page.

Review Activities

Choose the skills your student needs to review.

1. *Adverbs*
   Fill in the blank with an adverb of your choice.

   a. Describe how Jeremy ran.
      Jeremy ran _____ .
   b. Describe when Jeremy ran.
      Jeremy ran _____ .
   c. Describe where Jeremy ran.
      Jeremy ran _____ .

2. *Plural Nouns*
   Write the plural form for the following words.

   a. radio
   b. echo
   c. soprano
   d. foot
   e. mouse
   f. rodeo
   g. potato

3. *Paragraph*
   a. What do you call the main sentence of a paragraph?
   b. What do you call the other sentences that tell about the main idea?
   c. How do you begin a paragraph?

1. **Possible answers:**
   a. quickly, slowly, carefully, etc.
   b. yesterday, today, immediately, etc.
   c. inside, upstairs, etc.

2.
   a. radios
   b. echoes
   c. sopranos
   d. feet
   e. mice
   f. rodeos
   g. potatoes

3.
   a. topic sentence
   b. supporting sentences
   c. indent

Assessment 2
(Lessons 5 - 7)

1. Add capitalization.

   a. on saturday I will write robert a letter.
   b. last night I finished the book, <u>trumpet of the swan</u>.
   c. my family will visit my grandparents on thanksgiving.

2. Draw a vertical line to separate the complete subject and the complete predicate. Underline the simple subject once and underline the verb twice.

   a. The tired boys slept through the storm.
   b. Jonathan read a story.
   c. My friend had a birthday party.

3. Underline the adjectives and add commas.

   a. I ate a hot delicious apple pie.
   b. The room was filled with beautiful fresh flowers.
   c. My sister cut her silky long hair.

4. Add capitalization and punctuation to the following letter.

dear adam

   my mom told me you were sick. I hope you will be feeling better soon.

                    your friend
                    jim

1.
a. On Saturday I will write Robert a letter.
b. Last night I finished the book, <u>Trumpet of the Swan</u>.
c. My family will visit my grandparents on Thanksgiving.
2.
a. The tired <u>boys</u> / <u>slept</u> through the storm.
b. <u>Jonathan</u> / <u>read</u> a story.
c. My <u>friend</u> / <u>had</u> a birthday party.
3.
a. I ate a <u>hot</u>, <u>delicious</u> apple pie.
b. The room was filled with <u>beautiful</u>, <u>fresh</u> flowers.
c. My sister cut her <u>silky</u>, <u>long</u> hair.
4.

Dear Adam,

   My mom told me you were sick. I hope you will be feeling better soon.

                    Your friend,
                    Jim

5.
a. Present
b. Past
c. Past
d. Present

5. Read the following sentences. Tell if they are written in the present tense or past tense.

   a. The dog eats his food.
   b. Mom baked a cake.
   c. Dad fixed the door.
   d. The cat sleeps on the floor.

6.
a. ashes
b. monkeys
c. pennies
d. foxes
e. tables
f. teeth
g. tomatoes
h. stereos

6. Write the following nouns in its plural form.

   a. ash
   b. monkey
   c. penny
   d. fox
   e. table
   f. tooth
   g. tomato
   h. stereo

7.
a. The children played happily.
b. They laugh often.
c. The boys run around.

7. Underline the adverb in each sentence.

   a. The children played happily.
   b. They laugh often.
   c. The boys run around.

8. Indent

8. How do you begin a paragraph?

9. Topic Sentence

9. What is the main sentence of a paragraph called?

10. Supporting sentences

10. What are the sentences which tell about the main idea called?

Oral Presentations

and

Tall Tales

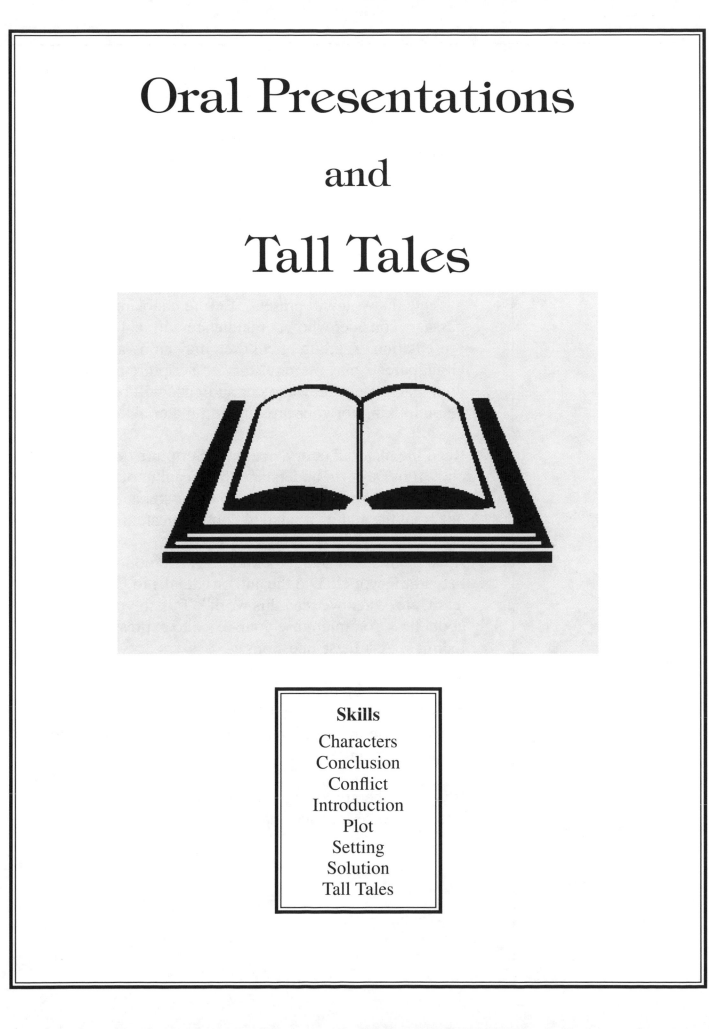

Skills

Characters
Conclusion
Conflict
Introduction
Plot
Setting
Solution
Tall Tales

Oral Presentation

1. Does your mother, father, or teacher read aloud to you? Talk to your teacher about the things you like and don't like about being read to by someone.

   This week you are going to prepare a read-aloud presentation for your family, class, or teacher.

   The first step is to choose the story, poem, or Scripture passage that you will present. Before choosing your passage, consider who your audience will be for the presentation. A group of children may enjoy a funny poem. Grandparents may prefer a story or Scripture passage. With your teacher, decide who your audience will be and then begin looking for your presentation material.

2. Read the material (story, poem, or Scripture) you have chosen in Day 1 to understand the meaning of it. Talk to your teacher about words you do not understand. Try to find out what the author wanted to communicate.

   Read the material again looking for the emotion (feelings) behind the words. Did the author want us to laugh, cry, learn, etc. when we read this work? Talk to your teacher about how you might use your voice to express these feelings. Ask these questions:

   1. What will I emphasize as I speak?
   2. Where will I pause as I speak?
   3. Will I use my voice in any other manner to communicate the meaning?

   If you will be presenting a story, you may need to use a different voice for each character.

3.- 4.

Practice reading your material aloud at least three times each day. You are not required to memorize the entire passage; however, you should know it well enough to be able to look up from your book several times during the presentation.

Stand in front of a mirror as you practice. Use the following list to help you evaluate yourself. After you have practiced several times, ask your teacher or another student to use the list to evaluate you.

Oral Presentation Checklist

_____ 1. Do I read slowly?
_____ 2. Do I read clearly?
_____ 3. Do I read loud enough?
_____ 4. Am I using my voice well to communicate the meaning and feeling?
_____ 5. Am I standing up straight, but naturally?
_____ 6. Do I look at my audience enough?

---

5. a. Your presentation day has arrived, and even though you may feel nervous, you are ready for your audience because you planned for it. If you feel very nervous, ask your teacher to sit in the back of the room and give you support by smiling at you.

Review Activities

1. Choose a Psalm or a segment of the poem, "Paul Revere's Ride" (page 25).

2. Read it silently once through.

3. Present an oral presentation.

Tall Tales

1. a. Listen as your teacher reads the story "Paul Bunyan and the Whistlin' River." Try to enjoy the type of language used to tell the story.

Paul Bunyan and The Whistlin' River
Retold by Linda Fowler

Maybe you've never heard of the Whistlin' River—but there was a time when it was known as the orneriest river ever to run between two banks. Some people say it was twisty and turny because it was always lookin' for trouble. Course, that was before the day it decided to get just a little too persnickety for its own good.

The Whistlin' River came by its name honestly, because every mornin' at 5:17 on the dot, and every evenin' at 6:22, just as regular as clock-work, it'd sit back on its haunches, draw itself up til it was about 203 feet tall, and let loose a piercing whistle that could be heard 679 miles away in every direction.

Now, if one man could haul a big load, it doesn't take a genius to figure that two men can haul twice as much. Likewise, if one man can hear, say, 20 miles, two men together ought to be able to hear twice as far right? So it was a regular practice for logging camps all the way up to Alaska to hire 2 or 12 men (as many as it took to hear the whistle without straining) whose main job was called "whistle-listener." That way everybody knew when to start work and when to quit, and all the camps ran smoothly (even on cloudy days).

One day, though, Paul Bunyan (who was really a gentle man, and not easily provoked) sat on a small mountain next to the Whistlin' River in deep thought. That river, who as I said before was well-known to be more ornery than most, took a notion it wanted to play. But Ol' Paul was workin' hard at figurin' a way to stack his bunkhouses in such a way that they wouldn't tip over when they were full of sleeping men, even if one or two had nightmares and started to toss and turn. This was important because, as it was, the logging camp was about the size of Galveston, Texas, and all those buildings scattered around kind of ruined the wilderness scenery. Stacking the bunkhouses when they were empty was easy. Taking them down to let the men in was easy, but keeping them in neat stacks once they were full of loggers was another thing entirely.

Anyhow, it was in the middle of all this pondering that the Whistlin' River all of a sudden hoisted itself up to a whopping 309 feet, leaned back just a little, and—pffffffffffffffttttttt—squirted about 4,287 gallons of water straight into Ol' Paul's beard. Now Paul was right proud of his beard, and took care to keep pine trees and trapped eagles and boulders combed out of it regularly–so he was not happy. But he figured that if he just ignored the river it'd go away, so he lowered his head and pretended nothing had happened.

Well, this did anything but discourage that overgrown stream of water, who immediately reared up to almost 402 and 1/2 feet, took a deep breath—and ppssssfffffffttt—let go a stream of water roughly the size of the Mississippi, complete with a batch of mud turtles, 77 large carp, and 2 very confused beavers.

That did it! Paul jumped up and let out a yell that set off a considerable landslide deep in the Rockies and startled a flock of ducks in Canada (who, as a result, arrived in the South months before they should've). "Well, I never!" said Paul, exclaiming and spitting all at the same time. "I declare I never saw such a fresh river!" he said. "Don't you know who you're squirting!" He stomped around, waving his arms, for a couple of hours—which totally tickled the Whistlin' River as it settled back into its banks with a contented sigh.

Eventually Paul got back to his deep thinkin', but this time his thoughts were on teaching that uppity river a lesson. It didn't take too long (about 2 days and 27 hours) for Ol' Paul, being a poetic sort of fellow, to decide that the best course of action would be to remove the river's kinks—which would naturally straighten it out. But even though his good friend Babe, the blue ox, was plenty strong enough to pull the twists and turns out of the river, it's a well-known fact that ordinary logging chains and skid hooks do not hold water. So he needed to figure out how in tarnation to hook Babe to the swollen stream, and that required a few more hours of heavy—VERY heavy—pondering.

When the idea finally dawned, it was so simple that Paul was ashamed he'd taken so long to think of it. That very minute he and Babe took out for the North Pole, covering the distance in long strides that caused wind-storms all along the way.

The closer they got to the Pole, the more blizzard tracks they began to see, and it wasn't long til Paul could tell they had reached the summer feeding grounds of all great winter storms. He lowered a sack of supplies from his shoulder and quickly set to constructing a huge box trap, which he carefully baited with fresh icicles. Then he and Babe tiptoed 40 or 50 miles back to enjoy their lunch and wait.

Wasn't long until they heard a commotion in the direction of their trap, but they waited just a little longer to make sure that whatever it was got caught for sure. Then they walked back quietly (so as not to spook their catch), peeked in, and were happy to see that they'd captured two very healthy half-grown blizzards. It was a little tricky gettin' those fellows into his sack, but Paul was determined. Then he and Babe raced back to camp in record time, (this time triggering windstorms that threatened to level whole towns along the way).

Before dinner that night, Paul tethered his young blizzards on either side of the pesky o' Whistlin' River, knowing full well they would do their job by morning. And sure enough, they did. When he strolled down to the riverbank after a light breakfast of two boxcars of sourdough pancakes (if ever a man loved flapjacks hot off the griddle, it was Paul Bunyan) and plenty of maple syrup, he found that river frozen solid.

From there, it was a simple thing to wrap a logging chain around the foot of the river about 51 times, hook the other end to Babe's harness, and holler at the Ox to "Pull!" That faithful animal, strong as it was, strained and grunted and groaned against the load. It dug its hooves into the ground and heaved with everything it had—but they didn't call that river ornery for nothing! It wouldn't budge.

Finally, Paul himself had to take hold of the chain and give it a good, strong yank. That, along with Babe's great strength, did the trick and the twisty, turny Whistlin' River was suddenly straight as a board. Course, this presented a new problem because with all the kinks out, the river was now three times longer than it had been.

Luckily, Paul had anticipated this turn of events and had already sent some of his men back to camp to fetch his great cross-cut saw and some baling wire. When they returned, he began sawing the river into 9-mile lengths, carefully rolling each section like linoleum and tying it with the wire. Now, all this truly did take some starch out of the Whistlin' River's attitude—some say it never mustered the gumption to whistle again. And even though loggers all over the country had to look for new ways to signal their startin' and quittin' times, in the end everybody benefited.

You see, over the next 50 or 60 years Paul took special care to deliver sections of river to any logging camp that had need of more water—for cooking, drinking, or floatin' logs to the mill. As a matter of fact, some say it was rolls from the Whistlin' River that made logging the forests of Texas possible—but that's another story.

    b. After listening, tell your teacher the answer to these questions:

        1) What is the **conflict** or (problem) that starts the story?
        2) How would you describe the Whistlin' River?
        3) How would you describe Paul Bunyan?
        4) How did Paul "straighten out" his problem?

1.
b. 1) The river squirts Paul Bunyan twice with water.
   2) ornery, troublecausing, playful
   3) big, strong, upset, poetic
   4) By making the Whistlin' River freeze, hooking it up to Babe with logging chains and pulling it straight.

c. The events of a story are called the **plot**. Choose one aspect of the plot to illustrate below, such as the Whistlin' River standing up, or Paul and Babe capturing the blizzards. If you do not wish to draw a picture, write a paragraph below describing what you would draw.

2. a. Read the story "Paul Bunyan and the Whistlin' River" silently. Now, narrate the story to your teacher. **Narration** is simply the retelling of an event.

   b. Find each of these words in your story. Read aloud the sentence that contains each word to your teacher. Using **context clues**, tell your teacher what you think each word means. (Refer to Lesson 6, **2c** for context clues.) If you can't come up with a definition, look up each word in the dictionary.

      1) gumption
      2) persnickety
      3) ornery

   c. Make up a new sentence using each word. Write each sentence and then use a **thesaurus** or dictionary to help you think of a **synonym**, or another word that is close in meaning to each of your words. Read your sentences, replacing the words with the synonyms.

3. a. Our story, "Paul Bunyan and the Whlstlin' River" is an example of a tall tale.

      Tall tales are a very important part of America's folk tradition. That is, they originated as simple stories told, and retold, by common people—sometimes about real "heroes," and sometimes not—but always about things, situations, or occupations that were well-known to the listeners. Characteristics found in just about all tall tales include humor, exaggeration, larger-than-life heroes, and use of phrases, words, and dialects common to the areas where the stories originated.

2.
b. 1) courage; nerve; initiative
   2) opinionated
   3) obstinate; having an ugly disposition

Each region of the country gave birth to its own set of tall tales: the eastern seaboard had Captain Stormalong and his great ship, the *Courser*; railroad workers sang about the mighty Casey Jones; the South-west and Mid-west celebrated John Henry and Mike Fink; and the West spun wild yarns about Pecos Bill and Davy Crockett. Of course, these are only a few of the many heroic legends made famous through tall tales, because America's folk tradition is as rich and varied as the country itself.

You may want to check the library for books or videos on tall tales.

b. Look over your story and find three or four examples of **exaggeration** and point them out to your teacher. One example is the description of the river squirting him with 4,287 gallons of water. That's a lot of water! Also talk with your teacher about what the author is trying to accomplish by using exaggeration in each case.

c. Talking with your teacher, come up with exaggerated descriptions to complete these phrases:

The tree was so tall it _____ .
The noise was as loud as _____ .

If you have any other tall tales that you can read, try to find more examples of exaggeration.

4. a. Yesterday, we looked at the element of exaggeration in tall tales. Another common element of tall tales is that the hero or heroine is larger-than-life. Another way to describe the main character is **super human**. Make a list of several of the things that Paul Bunyan does in our story that are larger-than-life.

b. The heroes or heroines of tall tales usually demonstrate qualities such as bravery, strength, and cleverness. Tell your teacher how Paul Bunyan showed his strength.

c. How did he show his cleverness?

3.
b. Possible answers:
1) ... 203 feet tall...
2) ... could,be heard 619 miles in every direction.
3) ... squirted 4,287 gallons of water ...
4) .. 8 light breakfast of 2 boxcars of sourdough pancakes.
5) ...he began sawing the river into 9 mile lengths ...
c. Possible Answers:
The tree was so tall it touched the sky.
The noise was as loud as a thousand airplanes.

4.
a. Possible answers:
1) ... let out a yell that set off a considerable landslide ...
2) ... covering the distance in long strides that caused windstorms ...
3) ... tiptoed 40 or 50 miles ...
b. Paul showed his strength by helping Babe pull the river straight.
c. Paul showed his cleverness by figuring out how to catch the blizzards.

d. Paul is opposed by the river itself.

e. Answers will vary.

5.

a. Possible answers:
1) ... squirted 4,287 gallons of water straight into Ol' Paul's beard.
2) ... Paul took care to keep pine trees and trapped eagles and boulders combed out of his beard regularly.
3) ... complete with a batch of mud turtles, 77 large carp, and 2 very confused beavers.

c. Thanks to Paul Bunyan delivering sections of the Whistlin' River to logging camps, the forest of Texas became a productive logging industry.

---

d. The hero/heroine of a tall tale always has a big problem to solve, or a strong foe to defeat. Tell about the force that opposes Paul in our story.

e. Do you think this foe would defeat a normal man?

5. a. Another common element of a tall tale is **humor**. If you have exaggeration, you are bound to have humor. The idea of someone eating two boxcars full of pancakes, or stacking bunkhouses can be pretty funny. Look over your story and find at least two examples of humor. List these examples on your paper and discuss them with your teacher.

b. Humor can be expressed in different ways. We can read something that is funny, we can say something humorous, or we can do something that brings a smile to our lips. Pretend you are Paul Bunyan. Act out some or all of the parts of the story for your family. You may want to dress like you think Paul Bunyan might have dressed. While you act out the story, tell the story from Paul Bunyan's point of view. For example, tell about when the river squirted you in the face and what you did about it.

c. Often, the end of a tall tale will provide a new explanation for why something is the way it is. What happens to the forest in Texas at the end of our story?

For the next two weeks, you are going to write your own tall tale. Take your time and enjoy your story.

We have already identified the elements of a tall tale in Lesson 9. They are: exaggeration, humor, and superhuman qualities of the hero or heroine. Another element of a tall tale is the language or **dialect** common to the area in which the story takes place. For example, in the West a phrase such as "Howdy, partner!" would be common. In the South, people might say "Hi, y'all." The language in a tall tale not only tells where the story takes place, it is also a reflection of the "color" and style of that area.

Step 1 - Think about your story.

As you begin to think about the story you want to write, talk to your teacher about these things:

1) the location (or setting) of your story
2) a hero or heroine
3) the problem your hero / heroine will face
4) equipping your hero / heroine with larger-than-life abilities
5) the exaggeration and humor you will use in your story
6) the conversation, or dialogue, you will use in your story
7) colorful descriptions and sayings that your hero / heroine can use

Step 2 - Brainstorm.

Use the Tall Tale Chart found on the next page, also on page 97 of the *Student Activity Book*, to make notes for your story. You or your teacher can fill out the chart as you talk about your story. Describe your hero/heroine, including superhuman qualities and exaggeration. Remember, the **setting**, or where the story takes place, can determine the dialect used in your story. Be sure to use a pencil as you brainstorm because you will probably change your mind as you talk about the story.

Step 3 - Make a list.

Your story will include several events. This is called the **plot**. On a blank sheet of paper, make a list of events that will occur in your story. You should write events that will bring about the **problem** that you wrote in the "Problem/Conflict" box of your Tall Tale chart, and that will bring about the **solution** that you wrote in the "Solution" box of your Tall Tale Chart. Use words or phrases. Be sure to number your list in the order the events will happen in the story.

Once you have decided on the characters and events of your story, you may begin drawing illustrations for each event. Draw each illustration on a separate sheet of white paper.

Tall Tale Chart

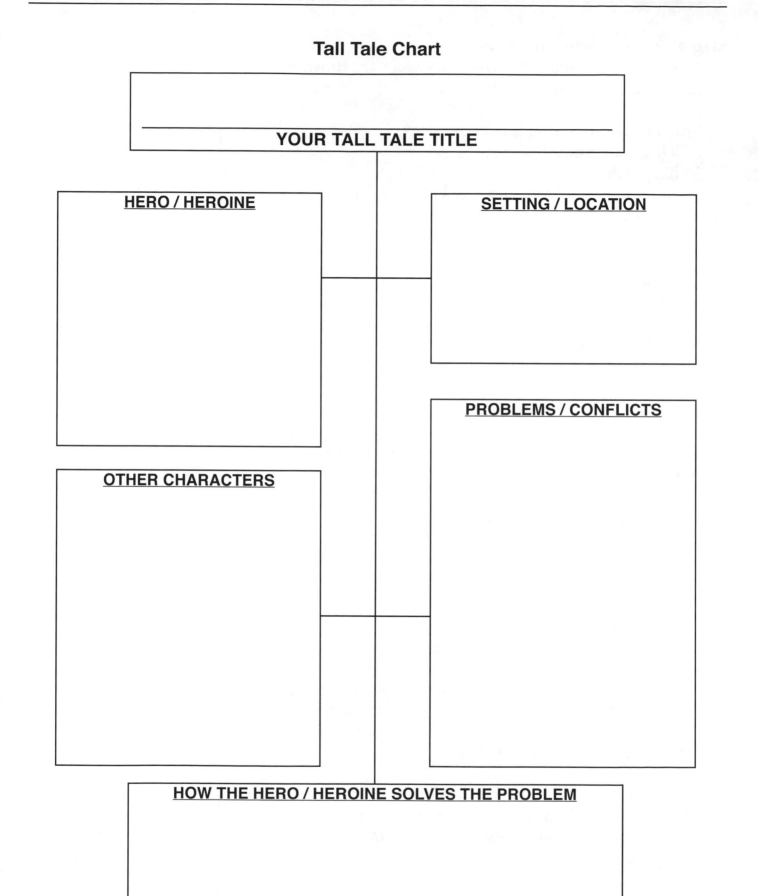

YOUR TALL TALE TITLE

HERO / HEROINE

SETTING / LOCATION

OTHER CHARACTERS

PROBLEMS / CONFLICTS

HOW THE HERO / HEROINE SOLVES THE PROBLEM

Step 4 - Begin writing.

You will need one piece of notebook paper for each event in the Problem section of your story. Use the first piece of paper for your first event. Begin writing about one third of the way down on your paper. Write two or three sentences describing the event, writing on every other line. Do the same for each of your other events.

Step 5 - Write topic sentences.

Each paragraph in your story will begin with a **topic sentence**. Reread one of your pages from **Step 4** describing an event in your story. What is the most important thing you want your reader to know about this event? Talk to your teacher about this most important thing.

On the top of your sheet, above the other sentences, write a sentence describing this most important thing. This is your topic sentence for the paragraph about this event.

Repeat this procedure for each event in your story. When you have completed this step, you will have written a paragraph for each event in your story.

Step 6 - Edit your paragraph.

Reread each one of your paragraphs. As you read, ask yourself these questions:

1) Can I describe a scene or person more fully?
2) Can I use **figurative language** in this paragraph?
   Ex: He was as mad as a bear with a toothache.
3) Can I include dialect in this paragraph?
4) Can I add exaggeration or humor in this event?

Step 7 - Write an introduction for your Tall Tale.

Read the first paragraph from our example "Paul Bunyan and the Whistlin' River," on page 77. The first paragraph of a story is called the **introduction**. Your introduction should help your readers get acquainted with the places and people in your story. Don't give away what the ending will be.

Step 8 - Write a conclusion for your story.
Bring the events and struggles to a close for your hero or heroine in the **conclusion** of your story. Remember, in tall tales, most heroes succeed in the end. Decide whether or not you want your hero to prevail. Use your imagination to make up a great ending.

Step 9 - Make a final copy of your story.
Rewrite or type your story, complete with a title, and the name of the author (you). Start with the introduction, then include the conflict and the solution in the order in which you determined they should occur. Lastly, write out your conclusion. Read your tall tale to yourself and enjoy it.

Step 10 - Present your Tall Tale.
Read your story to your family or class, or ask your teacher to read the story while you act it out. Illustrations make a nice addition to your story, so be sure to show your audience the illustrations you drew for each event (in Step 3). Put your story and illustrations in a folder, or staple them inside two pieces of construction paper for a cover. You'll want to share your tall tale with others in the years to come.

Review Activities

Choose the skills your student needs to review.

1. *Parts of a Story*

   a. What is the introduction of a story?
   b. What is the plot of a story?
   c. What is the conflict of a story?
   d. What is the solution of a story?
   e. What is the conclusion of a story?

2. What are some things that make up a tall tale?

1.
a. The introduction usually introduces the characters and setting.
b. The plot tells the events of a story.
c. The conflict is the problem in a story.
d. The solution solves the problem.
e. The conclusion tells the final thoughts of the story.

2. exaggeration, humor, super-human qualities, dialects

BOOK STUDY

on
The Trumpet of the Swan

The Trumpet of the Swan
by E. B. White
Published by Harper
Collins
Readability - 5th Grade

Introducing
The Trumpet of the Swan

Spark:
Can you for a moment imagine having no voice? How would you feel? How would you communicate? Try communicating some things to each other. *I'm hungry. You hurt my feelings. I'm scared. What time is it?*

Summary

Louis is a trumpeter swan born in the beautiful wilderness of Canada. Unlike his siblings, Louis is born without a voice. For trumpeter swans, this is a serious problem in finding a lifelong mate.

His father is determined to not let this little handicap keep his son from a normal and fulfilling life. Against his better judgement, his father breaks into a music store and steals a trumpet for Louis. He hopes that if Louis learns to play the trumpet, he may woo Serena, the beautiful swan Louis had long admired.

Louis feels badly that his father resorted to breaking the law, so he does everything he can to earn the money to repay the debt. With the help of his human friend, Sam Beaver, Louis learns to read and write as well as learn to play the trumpet.

All ends happily when the money is returned and Louis and Serena are united.

Vocabulary

Find the word in its context. Reread the sentences before and after the word. Do you understand the meaning of the word? Now, look up the word in the dictionary and write a clear, simple definition, and use it in a sentence.

1. treacherous (Chapter 1)

2. buoyant (Chapter 5)

3. serenity (Chapter 8)

4. extraordinary (Chapter 9)

5. triumphant (Chapter 19)

Complete the following sentences with the correct vocabulary word.

OR

Write your own sentences using the vocabulary words.

1. The swans enjoyed the _____ of the beautiful lakes.

2. The swamps can be _____ if you step into a soggy place.

3. After making his fame and fortune, Louis made a _____ return.

4. A swan is graceful and _____ in the water.

5. The swan crashing through the store window was an _____ event.

1. dangerous

2. able to float

3. peace

4. remarkable; beyond ordinary

5. successful; victorious

1. serenity

2. treacherous

3. triumphant

4. buoyant

5. extraordinary

1. Sam did not disturb the birds, but just watched them quietly from a distance. He also saw a fox creeping up towards the swan, and Sam threw a stick at him just in time.

2. Louis had no voice. He felt like he was different than his siblings. He felt frightened. He felt life was unjust and cruel to not have given him a voice.

3. Answers will vary. Make this an opportunity to focus on all the things your student can do.

4. Catastrophe means a disaster. Allow students to given their own definitions.

5. A good discussion should follow this question.

6. Applegate was upset and decided to go out in a canoe. This was against the rules; he had not passed his swimming test or his canoe test. A strong wind came and Applegate tipped over. He struggled in the water. The counsellors tried to rescue him but there was not enough time. Louis flew out to Applegate and picked him up on his back. Applegate was saved just in time.

Discussion Questions

Chapters 1 - 6

1. The swans were cautious of Sam at first. How did he become their friend? (Chapter 3)

2. What was Louis's problem and how did this make him feel? (Chapter 5)

3. Although Louis could not speak, it did not stop him from learning to swim and fly. Is there something **you** can't do? Now, list **all** the things you **can** do. (Chapter 6)

Chapters 7 - 12

4. In class, Louis wrote the word "catastrophe" on the blackboard. Some of the students gave their definition of the word. Tell your teacher what you think "catastrophe" means. (Chapter 7)

5. Louis' father broke into a music store to steal a trumpet for his son. What do you think of his actions? (Chapter 9)

6. Tell me about the rescue of Applegate Skinner. (Chapter 12)

Chapters 13 - 18

7. At Camp Kookooskoos, Mr. Bicle added one more item for Louis to carry around his neck. Can you think of all the items which now hung around Louis' neck? (Chapter 13)

8. Why did Louis want Sam to cut his webbed foot? (Chapter 13)

Chapters 19 - 21

9. Louis and Serena had a problem. How did Sam help them? (Chapter 19)

10. Tell me what happened when Louis' father returned the stolen money to the music store. (Chapter 20)

7. Louis now had a trumpet, slate, chalk, medal, and moneybag around his neck.

8. With toes, Louis knew he would be able to play all kinds of music.

9. Sam convinced the Head Man at the zoo that it would be best not to clip Serena's wings.

10. A salesman in the music store saw Louis approaching and in fear, yelled to the storekeeper to grab his gun. The storekeeper fired some shots and Louis' father continued flying towards the storekeeper and gave him his money. Upon seeing a drop of his own blood, Louis's father fainted. After the policemen and ambulance arrive, everything is cleared up and the cob receives a band-aid on his "wound."

I.C.A.N. Assessment

for

Trumpet of the Swan - Book Study B

After the *Book Study* is completed, check off each **I.C.A.N.** objective with your teacher.

C I can **complete** my work.

—— I can be **creative**.

A I can be **accurate**.

—— I can do my work with a good **attitude**.

N I can do my work **neatly**.

EVERYDAY WORDS

in

The Trumpet
of the Swan

Skills

Antonym	Compound verb	Interjection
Commas in Direct address	Conjunction	Preposition
Comparing adjectives	Contractions	Parts of a letter
Compound Sentence	Homonym	Quotation

Teacher's Note: As your student completes each lesson, choose skills from the Review Activities that he needs. The Review Activities follow each lesson.

"Well," said the cob, I guess it's no use. I guess you are dumb."
When he heard the word "dumb," Louis felt like crying. The cob saw that he had hurt Louis's feelings. "You misunderstand me, my son," he said in a comforting voice. "You failed to understand my use of the word 'dumb,' which has two meanings. If I had called you a dumb cluck or a dumb bunny, that would have meant that I had a poor opinion of your intelligence. Actually, I think you are perhaps the brightest, smartest, most intelligent of all my cygnets. Words sometimes have two meanings; the word 'dumb' is such a word. A person who can't speak is called dumb. That simply means he can't say anything. Do you understand?"

The Trumpet of the Swan by E.B. White. Text ©1970 by E.B. White.
Selection reprinted by permission of Harper Collins Publishers.

1. a. Listen as your teacher reads the literature passage. Read the passage silently. Ask your teacher to help you with difficult words. When you are ready, read the passage out loud to your teacher. In your own words, tell your teacher what is happening in this passage. The retelling of an event is called **narration**.

   b. As your teacher reads the lines in bold print out loud, write them down. Compare your copy to the literature passage and make corrections.

   c. List four to six words that you should study for spelling this week, or use the following list of suggested words: heard, misunderstand, comforting, voice.

      The three most common ways of spelling the **/er/** sound are **er**, **ir**, and **ur**. There is one more, **ear**.

Spelling Tip
Some words like *earth*
with an /er/ sound are
spelled with **ear**.

d. Copy these words, and underline **ear**. Say the words
aloud as you write them.

heard	earl
earth	early
earn	pearl
learn	yearn

e. In the literature passage Louis misunderstood because
his father used a **homonym**. His father has given us
a definition of homonyms, or words that sound the
same, and are sometimes spelled the same but have two
different meanings. Write the homonym that was used
and write the two meanings.

f. Use a dictionary to look up at least two meanings for
these homonyms.

1) sound   3) squash   5) fly
2) pitch   4) pound   6) duck

Make sure to use these words carefully so you won't be
misunderstood!

2. a. Our literature passage provides part of an imagined
conversation between a father swan (called a cob) and his
son (a cygnet). The cygnet, named Louis, has a problem.
Talk with your teacher about the limitation that Louis has
and what we call his problem.

b. When writing conversation, or **dialogue**, quotation
marks are placed around the actual words spoken or
thought. Refer to the Quotation Rules on page 98 when
completing the following exercise.

1.
e. dumb - of poor
intelligence; unable to
speak.

✐ Teacher's Note: Some
grammar books refer to
these as homographs.

f. Possible answers:
1) something you can
hear; normal state
of being; a body of
water
2) to throw; a black
sticky substance
3) a vegetable; to
squeeze
4) a unit of measure;
animal shelter
5) an insect; to move
through the air
6) a water bird; to
lower the body

2.
a. A handicap - allow time
for discussion.

Quotation Rules

1. Begin quotations with a capital letter.

2. If the quote comes before the person who spoke and tells something, place a comma after the quote, before the closing quotation mark. If the quote comes after the person who spoke and tells something, place the comma after the person who spoke, before the opening quotation mark.
   Ex: "You misunderstand me," said the cob.
   The cob said, "You misunderstand me."

3. If the quote comes before the person who spoke and asks something, place the question mark after the quote, before the closing quotation mark. If the quote comes after the person who spoke and asks something, place the question mark after the quote, before the closing quotation mark.
   Ex: "Do you understand?" he asked.
   He asked, "Do you understand?"

4. If the quote comes before the person who spoke and shows strong emotion, place the exclamation mark after the quote, before the closing quotation mark. If the quote comes after the person who spoke and asks something, place the exclamation mark after the quote, before the closing quotation mark.
   Ex: "Well!" said the cob.
   The cob said, "Well!"

5. A quote separated by the person who spoke is called a **split quotation.** Begin the first part of a split quotation with a capital letter, and end with a comma. Begin the second part of a split quotation with a lower case letter. Enclose both parts of the split quotation with quotation marks.
   Ex: "Tomorrow," said the cob, "we will visit my friends."

c. Add punctuation and capitalization.
1) sam asked when are we coming back
2) where is louis asked mr beaver
3) what will I do without a voice thought louis
4) his father said its time for bed
5) watch me said the mother swan and do everything I do
6) call the police yelled the salesgirl
7) some people talk said the cob but never listen

d. Together with your teacher, make a list of two or three possible problems that might be faced by a swan without a voice. What kind of problems might be faced by a person who can't speak? Make a list of four or five of the possible problems of a person who can't speak. Do you think a person who can't speak likes to be called *dumb*? Look up the word *mute*. Do you think they would prefer to be called *mute*?

3. a. Look at the sixth sentence in the second paragraph of the literature passage. Why is a comma used after *brightest* and *smartest*?

b. Adjectives like *bright*, *smart*, and *intelligent* can be described in degrees. If you compare two cygnets, you would say one cygnet is *brighter* than the other cygnet. This is called the **comparative degree**. If you compared three or more cygnets, you would say one cygnet was the *brightest* of all of them. This is called the **superlative degree**.

Complete the chart.

	Positive	Comparative	Superlative
Ex:	bright	brighter	brightest
	smart		
	happy		
	sweet		
	dark		
	clean		

2.
c. 1) Sam asked, "When are we coming back?"
2) "Where is Louis?" asked Mr. Beaver.
3) "What will I do without a voice?" thought Louis.
4) His father said, "It's time for bed."
5) "Watch me," said the mother swan, "and do everything I do."
6) "Call the police!" yelled the salesgirl.
7) "Some people talk," said the cob, "but never listen."

d. Answers will vary

3.
a. A comma is used to separate two or more adjectives.

b. Comparative Superlative
smarter   smartest
happier   happiest
sweeter   sweetest
darker   darkest
cleaner   cleanest

c. The adjective below, *intelligent*, is different than the adjectives used in the chart on page 99. You do not say one person is *intelligenter* than another. It sounds awkward and doesn't make sense. Often, words of three or more syllables will form the comparative by using the word *more*; and form the superlative by using the word *most*.

d. Complete the chart.

	Positive	Comparative	Superlative
Ex:	intelligent	more intelligent	most intelligent
	beautiful		
	magnificent		
	horrible		
	delightful		
	wonderful		

3.
d. Comparative
   more beautiful
   more magnificent
   more horrible
   more delightful
   more wonderful

   Superlative
   most beautiful
   most magnificent
   most horrible
   most delightful
   most wonderful

e. Some words may be formed with **-er** and -est; or with *more* and *most*.
   Ex: lovely - lovelier - loveliest
   OR   lovely - more lovely - most lovely

   However, do not use **-er** or **-est** with *more* or *most*.
   Ex: more lovelier; most loveliest - incorrect

f. Review your spelling words.

4. a. Look at the first sentence in the literature passage. The first word in the sentence, *well*, shows strong emotion. This is called an **interjection**.

List of Common Interjections		
well	oh	my
ohdear		wow

   Separate an interjection with a comma or an exclamation mark.
   Ex: Well, it's no use.
        Well, it's no use!
        Well! It's no use. (If you use an exclamation mark after the interjection, begin the next word with a capital letter.)

b. Rewrite the first sentence of the literature passage using an exclamation mark after the interjection.

c. Complete the sentences with interjections, and add punctuation and capitalization.
   1) wow I saw a swan nest with five eggs
   2) oh I have a present for you
   3) my look at the beautiful swan
   4) hey look over here
   5) well the boy did not laugh

d. Louis wrongly understood what his father meant. Look at the word *misunderstand*, and tell how you think the meaning of the word *understand* was changed to make the word *misunderstand*. Was something added?

e. A letter, or letters, added to the beginning of a word that changes its meaning is called a **prefix**. Specific prefixes change the meanings of words in specific ways. Prefixes are not always words by themselves, but usually make an additional syllable, or sound, when added to the base word. Think of it as a building. The **base word** is the original house. Prefixes are parts that are added to the front of the house that change the meaning, like a garage.

The house is larger now, and can be used for more things. So, your original word can be used in new ways because of the prefix. The prefix **mis-** means *wrongly*. Look at the list of words and make new words by adding the prefix **mis**.

mis   understood

spell   count   read   place

f. Write sentences using each of your new words.

g. Optional: Take an oral or written spelling pretest.

4.
b. "Well!" said the cob. "I guess it's no use. I guess you are dumb."

c. 1) Wow! I saw a swan nest with five eggs. or Wow, I saw a swan nest with five eggs!
   2) Oh, I have a present for you! or Oh! I have a present for you.
   3) My, look at the beautiful swan! or My! Look at the beautiful swan
   4) Hey! Look over here. or Hey, look over here!
   5) Well, the boy did not laugh! or Well! The boy did not laugh.

d. Yes, the letters mis.

e. misspell   miscount
   misread   misplace

f. Possible Answers:
   1) He will practice spelling words so he won't *misspell* them.
   2) You will get a wrong answer if you *miscount*.
   3) Look at the letters carefully so you won't *misread* them.
   4) Did he *misplace* the map?

5. a. Listen as your teacher reads the literature passage for dictation. Do not write as it is read the first time. Just listen. Remember, writing from dictation is a skill you acquire with practice, like hitting a baseball. Your first attempts may not be too successful, but as you practice you will become better.

   b. After you listen to the literature passage the second time, write what you have heard. When you have finished, compare your copy to the literature passage.

   c. Optional: Take a spelling test.

   d. Optional: Choose skills from the *Review Activities* on the next page.

Review Activities

Choose the skills your student needs to review.

1. *Quotations*
   Add capitalization and punctuation.

   a. where are my books asked tom
   b. your books are on the desk said mom where you left them
   c. tom asked where is my pencil
   d. mom sighed your pencil is in your bookbag
   e. there's a phone call for you yelled sara
   f. travis asked who is it

2. *Base Word / Prefix* **mis-**
   Circle the base word and underline the prefix.

   a. mislead
   b. misinform
   c. misfire
   d. misunderstand
   e. misprint

3. *Homonym*
   Tell what the italicized word means in each sentence.

   a. *Pound* can mean an animal shelter; or a unit of measure. Write two sentences using the homonyms of both meanings.

   b. *Down* can mean the opposite of up; or soft feathers of a young bird. Write two sentences using the homonyms of both meanings.

4. *Adjectives / Comparative and Superlative*
   Complete the chart.

Positive	Comparative	Superlative
a. quiet		
b. stiff		
c. fast		
d. fun		
e. useful		
f. splendid		

1.
a. "Where are my books?" asked Tom.
b. "Your books are on the desk," said Mom, "where you left them."
c. Tom asked, "Where is my pencil?"
d. Mom sighed, "Your pencil is in your bookbag."
e. "There's a phone call for you!" yelled Sara.
f. Travis asked, "Who is it?"

2.
a. mis (lead)
b. mis (inform)
c. mis (fire)
d. mis (understand)
e. mis (print)

3. Possible Answers:
a. My father bought a puppy from the pound. Mother bought a pound of butter.
b. I sleep with a down comforter in the winter. The ball fell down.

4. Comparative
   a. quieter
   b. stiffer
   c. faster
   d. more fun
   e. more useful
   f. more splendid

   Superlative
   a. quietest
   b. stiffest
   c. fastest
   d. most fun
   e. most useful
   f. most splendid

5.
8. Oh
b. Wow
c. Oh my
d. Well
e. Oh

6. wrongly

5. *Interjections*
   Underline the interjections.

   a. Oh, I forgot to call you!
   b. Wow, I've never seen that before!
   c. Oh my, Ronnie will like that!
   d. Well, it's good to see you again.
   e. Oh! Come see the sunset!

6. What does the prefix **mis-** mean?

"Do not let an unnatural sadness settle over you, Louis," said the cob. *"Swans must be cheerful, not sad; graceful, not awkward; brave, not cowardly.* **Remember that the world is full of youngsters who have some sort of handicap that they must overcome. You apparently have a speech defect. I am sure you will overcome it, in time.** *There may even be some slight advantage, at your age, in not being able say anything. It compels you to be a good listener. The world is full of talkers, but it is rare to find anyone who listens."*

The Trumpet of the Swan by E.B. White. Text ©1970 by E.B. White. Selection reprinted by permission of Harper Collins Publishers.

Teacher's Note: As your student completes each lesson, choose skills from the Review Activities that he needs. The Review Activities follow each lesson.

1. a. Read the literature passage silently. Ask your teacher to help you with difficult words. When you are ready, read the passage out loud to your teacher. Narrate to your teacher what is happening in this passage.

   b. As your teacher reads the lines in bold print out loud, write them down. Compare your copy to the literature passage and make corrections.

   c. List four to six words that you should study for spelling this week, or use the following list of suggested words: full, apparently, defect, world.

   When you spell a one-syllable word like *full* which ends with a single short vowel and **l, f, s** or **z**, you often double the last consonant.

   ```
   Spelling Tip
   One syllable words ending in a single
   short vowel and l, f, s, and z, are often
   spelled with a double consonant.
   ```

2.

a. Louis

b. A comma

c. 1) Serena, you are the most beautiful swan.
2) You, Serena, are the most beautiful swan.
3) You are the most beautiful swan, Serena.
4) Louis, you must keep your head up.
5) You, Louis, must keep your head up.
6) You must keep your head up, Louis.

d. Copy these words, and underline the double consonants. Say the words aloud as you write them.

pass   mess
huff   cuff
doll   pill
jazz   fizz

2. a. Look at the first sentence of the literature passage. To whom is the cob speaking?

b. What punctuation mark is used before the word, *Louis*? When addressing someone, separate the person spoken to with commas.
Ex: Do not be sad, Louis.
Louis, do not be sad.
Be cheerful, Louis, not sad.

c. Add commas.
1) Serena you are the most beautiful swan.
2) You Serena are the most beautiful swan.
3) You are the most beautiful swan Serena.
4) Louis you must keep your head up.
5) You Louis must keep your head up.
6) You must keep your head up Louis.

d. Look at the last sentence of the literature passage. The word after the comma is *but*. The word *but* is a conjunction. **Conjunctions** are joining words. Conjunctions can join words, phrases, or sentences.

List of Common Conjunctions	
and	but
or	so

In this sentence, the conjunction *but* joins two sentences. The first part of the sentence, *The world is full of talkers*, is a complete sentence. *It is rare to find anyone who listens* is also a complete sentence. Two sentences joined together with a conjunction is called a **compound sentence**.

Separate a compound sentence with a comma <u>before</u> the conjunction.

Ex: You have a speech defect, but you will overcome it.
      You have a speech defect. - This is a complete
      sentence. It has a subject and a predicate.
      You will overcome it. - This is a complete
      sentence. It has a subject and a predicate.

e. Look at the following sentences:
    Dinner is ready. I am hungry.

    You can join these two sentences with a comma and a
    conjunction and make one sentence:
    Dinner is ready, and I am hungry.

f. Rewrite the following sentences into compound sentences.
    Choose the best conjunction.
    1) Louis swam around. He sang to Serena.
    2) Sam wanted to stay with the cygnets. He went home.
    3) Louis could not speak. So he learned to read and write.
    4) I must take my chance now. I will never do it.
    5) Louis knew what he had to do. He flew out to the boy.

3. a. In the second sentence of our literature passage there are
       three pairs of words that are opposites, or **antonyms**.
       The way these words are used in this sentence show
       comparisons between one thing and another. Underline
       the word pairs in the second sentence that are opposites.

   b. The last two sentences of our literature passage also have
       a pair of words that are opposites. Find this word pair
       and underline them.

   c. Why do you think the cob is using words that are opposites?

   d. Do you think it will help Louis understand?

   e. In your own words rewrite the advice given in this
       passage. Encourage Louis with the same ideas that his
       father has used, but don't use the same words. Talk about
       your ideas with your teacher before you write.

   f. Review your spelling words.

2.
e. Possible answers:
   1) **Louis swam around, and he sang to Serena.**
   2) **Sam wanted to stay with the cygnets, but he went home.**
   3) **Louis could not speak, so he learned to read and write.**
   4) **I must take my chance now, or I will never do it.**
   S) **Louis knew what he had to do, so he flew out to the boy.**

3.
a. **cheerful-sad, graceful-awkward, brave-cowardly**
b. **listener-talker**

c. **to provide a clear contrast between right and wrong**

d. **Answers will vary.**

e. **Answers will vary.**

4. a. When an ending is added to a base or root word, it changes the meaning of the word. Remember the picture we used to show base words? The main house is the base word, and the extra room on the right is a **suffix**. Here's an example:

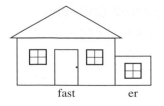

fast   er

4.

b. cheerful, graceful

b. Find the words in the literature passage with the ending **-ful** added to them and write them down.

c. It adds one syllable.

c. How many syllables, or sounds, does the suffix **-ful** add to each word?

d. It means to be full of.

d, The two **-ful** words in our literature passage are *cheerful* and *graceful*. What do you think the suffix **-ful** means?

e. cheerful- full of cheer
graceful - full of grace

e. Tell your teacher what you think these words mean. If you are unsure, look them up in the dictionary.

f. 1) full of play
2) full of beauty
3) full of care or caution

f. Read this list of words and write down what you think they mean.
1) playful
2) beautiful
3) careful

g. Look at these words:
arm - armful   care - careful
beauty - beautiful   play - playful

g. When the base word ends in a consonant and y, drop the y before adding the suffix -ful.

When do changes in spelling need to be made, and what changes do you make?

h. colorful
joyful
bountiful

h. Add the suffix **-ful** to these words and write a sentence using each one.
color   joy   bounty

i. Optional: Take an oral or written spelling pretest.

5. a. Listen as your teacher reads the literature passage for dictation. Do not write as it is read the first time. Just listen. Remember, writing from dictation is a skill you acquire with practice, like hitting a baseball. Your first attempts may not be too successful, but as you practice you will become better.

   b. After you listen to the literature passage the second time, write what you have heard. When you have finished, compare your copy to the literature passage.

   c. Optional: Take a spelling test.

   d. Optional: Choose skills from the Review Activities on the next page.

1.
a. Justin, please come here.
b. Can you help us, Robert?
c. Hopefully, Sara, we will go on vacation.
d. Amanda, I'm going home.
e. Please come with me, Beth.
f. I can't, Amanda, because I'm doing my homework.

2.
a. Jerry likes to play baseball, but I like to play football.
b. The moon shone, and the stars twinkled.
c. Karla runs fast, but Sal runs slowly.
d. Amy slept in the tent, and (or but) I slept outside.

3. Possible answers:
a. timid, cowardly
b. dirty, impure, polluted
c. moist, wet, damp
d. hard, rigid, firm
e. top, peak, summit
f. smooth, coarse, harsh

4.
a. softer
b. nicer
c. kinder
d. fresher
e. quicker
f. taller

5.
a. plentiful
b. spoonful
c. hopeful
d. mOiJithful
e. pitiful
f. boutifiJil

Review Activities

Choose the skills your student needs to review.

1. *Commas / Direct Address*
   Place commas correctly in the following sentences.

   a. Justin please come here.
   b. Can you help us Robert?
   c. Hopefully Sara we will go on vacation.
   d. Amanda I'm going home.
   e. Please come with me Beth.
   f. I can't Amanda because I'm doing my homework.

2. *Compound Sentence / Conjunction / Commas*
   Make compound sentences.

   a. Jerry likes to play baseball. I like to play football.
   b. The moon shone. The stars twinkled.
   c. Karla runs fast. Sal runs slowly.
   d. Amy slept in the tent. I slept outside.

3. *Antonyms*
   Write antonyms for the following words.

   a. brave   b. clean
   c. dry   d. soft
   e. bottom   f rough

4. *Suffix -er*
   Add the suffix **-er** to the following words.

   a. soft   b. nice
   c. kind   d. fresh
   e. quick   f. tall

5. *Suffix -ful*
   Add the suffix **-ful** to the following words.

   a. plenty   b. spoon
   c. hope   d. mouth
   e. pity   f bounty

"There are mechanical devices that convert air into beautiful sounds. One such device is called a trumpet. I saw a trumpet once, in my travels. **I think you may need a trumpet in order to live a full life. I've never <u>known</u> a Trumpeter Swan to need a trumpet, but your case is different. I intend to get you what you need.** *I don't know how I will manage this, but in the fullness of time it shall be accomplished. And now that our talk has come to a close, let us return gracefully to the other end of the pond, where your mother and your brothers and sisters await us!"*

The Trumpet of the Swan by E.B. White. Text ©1970 by E.B. White. Selection reprinted by permission of Harper Collins Publishers.

✐ **Teacher's Note:** As your student completes each lesson, choose skills from the Review Activities that he needs. The Review Activities follow each lesson.

1. a. Read the literature passage silently. Ask your teacher to help you with difficult words. When you are ready, read the passage out loud to your teacher. In your own words, tell your teacher what is happening in this passage.

   b. As your teacher reads the lines in bold print out loud, write them down. Compare your copy to the literature passage and make corrections.

   c. List four to six words that you should study for spelling this week, or use the following list of suggested words: known, different, intend, trumpet.

   There are two common ways to spell a **/n/** sound using a silent letter: **kn** and **gn**. There is no rule to tell you which one to use, but it is helpful to get familiar with these words. However, **kn** will usually not end a word.

Spelling Tip
There are two common ways to spell a **/n/** sound using a silent letter: **kn** and **gn**, but **kn** will usually not end a word.

---

d. Copy these words, and underline **kn** and **gn**. Say the words aloud as you write them.

kn	**gn**
know	gnaw
knot	gnat
knowledge	gnome
knew	reign
knapsack	sovereign
knit	benign
knead	foreign

2.
a. don't

2. a. Look at the second bolded sentence in the literature passage. The first word is *I've*. This is a shortened way of saying *I have*. The apostrophe takes the place of the missing letters, **ha**. This is called a **contraction**. Find the other contraction in the literature passage.

b. do not

b. What does it stand for?

c. the letter "o"

c. What does the apostrophe take the place of?

d. 1) I would
2) they will
3) must not
4) you are
5) she would (had)
6) they are
7) it will
8) are not
9) it is
10) he is

d. Write the words these contractions stand for.
1)	I'd	6)	they're
2)	they'll	7)	it'll
3)	mustn't	8)	aren't
4)	you're	9)	it's
5)	she'd	10)	he's

e. The contraction *it's* stands for *it is*. This contraction is often confused with the possessive pronoun, *its*.
Ex: *It's* time to go. (It is time to go.)
      The monkey hung by *its* tail. (The tail belongs to the monkey.)

2.
e. 1) It's
2) its
3) It's
4) It's
5) Its

Complete the sentences with the correct word. (it's / its)
1) _____ almost noon.
2) The tree spread out _____ branches.
3) I hope _____ nice.
4) _____ in Canada.
5) The cygnet pulled the shoestring from _____ place.

f. *You're* is another contraction. This is also often confused with the possessive pronoun, *your*.
    Ex: *You're* late for dinner. (You are late for dinner.)
         John, did you bring *your* books? (The books belong to John.)

    Complete the sentences with the correct word.
    (you're / your)
    1) Get _____ trumpet.
    2) I think _____ nice.
    3) I think _____ trumpet is clear and crisp.
    4) Here is _____ medal.
    5) _____ going to camp with me.

f. 1) your
    2) you're
    3) your
    4) your
    5) You're

g. *They're* is another contraction. This contraction is often confused with the possessive pronoun *their* and the word *there*.

    Ex: *They're* coming to visit. (They are coming to visit.)
         I hope Aunt Judy and Uncle Bob bring *their* pictures.
         (The pictures belong to Aunt Judy and Uncle Bob)
         There is an alligator at the zoo.

    Complete the sentences with the correct word.
    (they're / their / there)
    1) _____ was a job for Louis in the city.
    2) The boys brought _____ sleeping bags to camp.
    3) _____ going canoeing in the morning.
    4) The boys swam _____ to listen.
    5) Mr. and Mrs. Beaver loved _____ son.

g. 1) There
    2) their
    3) They're
    4) there
    5) their

h. Look at the last sentence of the literature passage. Find the word that ends in **-ly**.

h. gracefully

i. What is the base or root word of *gracefully*? What part of speech is *grace*?

i. grace; noun

j. What part of speech is the word when the suffix **-ful** is added? Serema is a *graceful* swan.

j. adjective

k. adverb

k. What part of speech is the word when the suffix **-ly** is added to that new word? She swam *gracefully*.

Hint
Most words ending in **-ly** are adverbs. Some exceptions are *friendly* and *lovely* which are adjectives.

l. quickly   sadly
   brightly   slowly
   loudly   bravely

l. Copy the list of words and add **-ly** to the end of each word.
   quick   sad   bright
   slow   loud   brave

m. Answers will vary.

m. Write sentences using at least three of the new words.

3. a. So far, you have learned seven parts of speech: noun, verb, pronoun, adjective, adverb, conjunction, and interjection. The last part of speech you will learn is the preposition.

List of Common Prepositions			
above	under	in	into
around	over	to	against
after	along	beneath	below
behind	by	from	toward
with	through	on	

Prepositions show the relationship between the noun which follows the preposition and another word in the sentence. The preposition with the noun is called a **prepositional phrase**.

Ex: The cat ran around the house.
      Around is the preposition. It shows the relationship between *house* and *cat*.
      Around the house is the prepositional phrase.

b. Look at the first sentence in the literature passage. Can you find the prepositional phrase? If you have a hard time, look at the list of prepositions. Underline the prepositional phrase and circle the preposition.

c. Now, look at the third sentence in the literature passage. Underline the prepositional phrase and circle the preposition.

d. Look at the pictures and complete the sentences using a prepositional phrase. Circle the preposition.

1) The rabbit scurried _____.

2) The kite is flying _____.

3) The boy is standing _____.

4) The girl is sleeping _____.

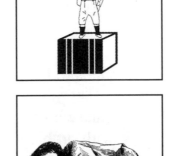

e. In our literature passage, there are several words which look the same, and are pronounced the same, but have more than one meaning. These words are called homonyms. One of these words is *case* which can mean either a *situation* or a *carton*. How do you know which definition is being used in our passage?

3.
b. (into) beautiful sounds

c. (in) my travels

d. **Possible Answers:**
   1) (under) the fence.
   2) (over) the house.
   3) (on) a box.
   4) (on) the bed

e. The context, or other sentences help us know which meaning is being used.

✎ Teacher's Note: Some grammar books refer to these words as homographs.

3.
f. saw
    Possible Answers:
    I *saw* a trumpet.
    The carpenter uses a
    saw.

g. Possible answers:
1) David hit the ball with
    the bat. The bat flew
    from the attic.
2) The boy bounced the
    ball. Cinderella went to
    the ball.
3) I filled the pitcher with
    juice. The pitcher
    threw a curveball.
4) Turn off the light.
    We had a light rain this
    morning.

4.
a. Answers will vary.

b. By getting Louis a
    trumpet

c. Allow for discussion.

f. Look at the third sentence in the literature passage. Can you find the homonym?

Write two sentences using the different meanings for that word.

g. Do you know the different meanings for the following words? You may use a dictionary if needed. Write sentences for the different meanings of these words.
    1) bat
    2) ball
    3) pitcher
    4) light

4. a. The cob has brought a problem to his son's attention. Louis probably wasn't very aware of his differences from the other cygnets, but now he is more aware. This will probably make Louis feel uncomfortable, but may be the beginning of learning how to cope with problems. Talk with your parent about problems that you have been made aware of about yourself, or a problem they were made aware of as children. How did they deal with their problems? How have you tried to cope with differences you might feel?

b. Part of helping with a problem is making the person aware of it. Another part is helping the person find a way to solve the problem. Tell your teacher how Louis' father plans to help Louis.

c. Talk with your teacher about specific ways to help people with problems such as blindness, deafness, or physical impairments. These are devices that have been designed especially to help these people do things that would otherwise be hard.

It used to be thought that people were born with physical or mental limitations as a punishment from God toward the parents. As a result, people often hid family members who were handicapped. Do you think people who are handicapped are being punished by God? Talk with your parents about what you believe.

Realizing that everyone has some sort of obstacle to overcome, think about the meaning of these Scriptures and how you can apply them when relating to people with limitations.

John 9:1-3   Psalm 139:14-16

5. a. Listen as your teacher reads the literature passage for dictation. Do not write as it is read the first time, just listen. Remember, writing from dictation is a skill you acquire with practice, like hitting a baseball. Your first attempts may not be too successful, but as you practice you will become better.

   b. After you listen to the literature passage the second time, write what you have heard. When you have finished, compare your copy to the literature passage.

   c. Optional: Take a spelling test.

   d. Optional: Choose skills from the *Review Activities* on the next page.

Review Activities

Choose the skills your student needs to review.

1.

a. she'll
b. you've
c. I'd
d. they're
e. he's
f. isn't
g. couldn't
h. can't

1. *Contractions*
   Write the contraction for the following words.

   a. she will   e. he is
   b. you have   f. is not
   c. I would   g. could not
   d. they are   h. can not

2.

a. It's
b. you're
c. their
d. its
e. your
f. they're
g. There

2. *(It's / its) (your / you're) (their / there/ they're)*
   Choose the correct word.

   a. _____ raining today.
   b. I hope _____ well.
   c. The boys will bring _____ trading cards.
   d. We watched the kitten chase _____ tail.
   e. Give the flowers to _____ mother.
   f. I hope _____ what she likes.
   g. _____ are other flowers to choose from.

3.

a. quickly -The horse galloped quickly.
b. silently -The baby rested silently.
c. carefully - Sara polished the furniture carefully.
d. stubbornly -The donkey brayed stubbornly.

3. *Adverb - Suffix -ly*
   Add the suffix **-ly** to the following adjectives to make adverbs. Use each word in a sentence.

   a. quick
   b. silent
   c. careful
   d. stubborn

4.

a. on the floor.
b. up the hill.
c. under the bridge.
d. after the bus.
e. by the river.

4. *Prepositions*
   Underline the prepositional phrase and circle the preposition.

   a. The toddler fell on the floor.
   b. The old man walked up the hill.
   c. The ship went under the bridge.
   d. The woman ran after the bus.
   e. I sat by the river.

The cob turned and swam off. Louis followed. It had been an unhappy morning for him. He felt frightened at being different from his brothers and sisters. It scared him to be different. He couldn't understand why he had come into the world without a voice. Everyone else seemed to have a voice. Why didn't he? "Fate is cruel," he thought. "Fate is cruel to me." Then he remembered that his father had promised to help, and he felt better.

The Trumpet of the Swan by E.B. White. Text ©1970 by E.B. White.
Selection reprinted by permission of Harper Collins Publishers.

✎ **Teacher's Note:** As your student completes each lesson, choose skills from the Review Activities that he needs. The Review Activities follow each lesson.

1. a. Read the literature passage silently. Ask your teacher to help you with difficult words. When you are ready, read the passage out loud to your teacher. Narrate to your teacher what is happening in this passage.

   b. As your teacher reads the lines in bold print out loud, write them down. Compare your copy to the literature passage and make corrections.

   c. List four to six words that you should study for spelling this week, or use the following list of suggested words: followed, frightened, different, turned.

   The three most common ways of spelling words with an **/er/** sound are **er**, **ir**, and **ur**.

Spelling Tip
er in her
ir in sir
ur in burn

   Copy these words, and underline **er**, **ir**, and **ur**.

er	**ir**	**ur**
her	first	turned
teacher	third	churn
term	bird	purpose
perky	dirt	Thursday

2.

a. cob

b. turned, swam

c. Then he remembered that his father had promised to help, and he felt better.

d. Possible answers
   1) swam and played
   2) spoke and planned
   3) talked and gazed

e. "Fate is cruel."
   "Fate is cruel to me."

f. Answers will vary.

3.
a. Answers will vary.

3.
b. Louis felt comforted when he remembered his father's promise.

2. a. Look at the first sentence of the literature passage. What is the subject?

   b. What are the verbs?

   The subject, *cob* did two things. He *turned* and *swam*. This is called a **compound verb**. Two verbs are joined by the **conjunction** *and*. Do not confuse this with a compound sentence. *The cob turned* is a complete sentence. But *swam off* is not a complete sentence. It lacks a subject.

   c. Can you find the compound sentence in the literature passage?

   d. Complete the sentence by adding a compound verb.
      1) Louis _____ and _____ .
      2) His father _____ and _____ .
      3) Serena _____ and _____ .

   e. Read aloud the actual words thought by Louis. Remember, quotation marks enclose the actual words spoken or thought.

   f. Write something you have thought about.
      Ex: "How wonderful it would be to fly," I thought.

3. a. Louis feels afraid because he now realizes how different he is from the other cygnets. Do you think that this is an understandable feeling for Louis? Can you think of any situations where you felt very different from everyone else? What did you do? Did it change the way you acted? Talk with your teach about that situation.

   b. Ask your teacher if she has ever had to deal with feeling very different from everyone else. Ask her how she handled the situation, and what advice she would give you to keep in mind if you have to face a similar situation. Read the last line of our literature passage. Tell how Louis felt about his father's promise.

c. Look back at each literature passage from *The Trumpet of the Swan* (Lessons 12-15). Each passage contains statements from Louis's father that tells what he thinks of Louis and what he will do to help him. Write a friendly letter to Louis and tell him what his father thinks of him, and how he will help. Use the sample letter below to help you write a friendly letter.

(Date)
February 10, 1997

(Greetings or salutation)
Dear Sally,

    I heard that you broke your leg skateboarding last week. I hope it doesn't hurt too much! I know there are many things you cannot do with your leg in a cast.
    I will be happy to return your books to the library. If there's anything else I can do, please call me. You are a good friend and I want to help you.   (body)

(closing)
Your friend,
(Signature)
Mary

---

4. a. In our literature passage, Louis talks about something called *fate*. Look up this word in the dictionary and tell your teacher the definition. If you do not know what the word *cruel* means, look that up, too. What does Louis mean by the statement, "Fate is cruel to me."?

   b. Do you believe that fate controls your life? Talk with your teacher about your answer, and ask her what she believes. Why do you think Louis believes that fate caused him not to have a voice?

   c. Listen as your teacher reads Psalm 139:14-16. The author of this psalm is David. Do you think David believes that fate is controlling his life? Who does David believe has ordained his days?

4.
a. Possible answer: The plan for my life is unkind to me, and there is nothing I can do to change it.

b. Answers will vary.

c. No
God

5. a. Listen as your teacher reads the literature passage for dictation. Do not write as it is read the first time, just listen. Remember, writing from dictation is a skill you acquire with practice, like hitting a baseball. Your first attempts may not be too successful, but as you practice you will become better.

   b. When you have finished, compare your copy to the literature passage.

   c. Optional: Take a spelling test. After you write each word, use it in a sentence orally.

   d. Optional: Choose skills from the *Review Activities* on the next page.

Review Activities

Choose the skills your student needs to review.

1. *Compound Verb*
   Rewrite the sentences to make one sentence with a compound verb.

   a. I worked. I played.
   b. Ashley likes drawing. Ashley likes painting.
   c. The baby laughed. The baby played.
   d. The family prayed together. The family sang together.

2. *Letters*
   Label the parts of a letter.

   ```
                         April 10, 1996

   Dear Paul,

        I hope you are feeling
   better after your illness.  I
   miss  seeing  you  at
   church.  I will call you to
   see when I can visit.

                    Your friend,
                    John
   ```

1.
a. I worked and played.
b. Ashley likes drawing and painting.
c. The baby laughed and played.
d. The family prayed and sang together.

2.

Date
Greeting or salutation
Body
Closing
Signature

1.

a. "Where is Dad?" asked Jerry.

b. "He is in the garage," said Sara.

c. Jerry said, "Someone is here to see you, Dad."

2.

a. smaller, smallest

b. stronger, strongest

c. more beautiful, most beautiful

3.

a. <u>Well</u>, I'll try again.

b. <u>Wow</u>! Did you see that?

c. <u>My</u>, you have grown.

4.

a. Please open the door, Robert.

b. Mom, may I go out and play?

c. Tell me, Sara, if you are coming.

5.

a. Mom like cats, and Dad likes dogs.

b. I tried to be on time, but I was late.

c. Would you like ice cream, or would you like cake?

6. antonyms

Assessment 3
(Lessons 12 - 15)

1. Add capitalization and punctuation.

   a. where is Dad asked jerry

   b. he is in the garage said sara

   c. jerry said someone is here to see you, Dad.

2. Complete the chart.

Positive	Comparative	Superlative
a. small		
b. strong		
c. beautiful		

3. Underline the interjections.

   a. Well, I'll try again.

   b. Wow! Did you see that?

   c. My, you have grown.

4. Add commas.

   a. Please open the door robert.

   b. Mom may I go out and play?

   c. Tell me sara if you are coming.

5. Make compound sentences by adding a conjunction and a comma.

   a. Mom likes cats. Dad likes dogs.

   b. I tried to be on time. I was late.

   c. Would you like ice cream? Would you like cake?

6. The words *open* and *close* have opposite meanings. What are these kind of words called?

7. Write contractions for the following words.

   a. is not
   b. could not
   c. they are
   d. she will

8. Underline the prepositional phrase and circle the preposition.

   a. The log floated on the water.
   b. She sat on the chair.
   c. The bird flew over the roof.

9. Rewrite the sentences to make one sentence using a conjunction and a compound verb.

   a. I danced. I sang.
   b. The boy laughed. The boy played.
   c. The dog ran. The dog barked.

10. Label the parts of a letter.

February 10, 1997

Dear Grandma,

   Mom and Dad gave me a puppy for my birthday. He is so cute. I named him Rascal. Please come and see my new puppy.

                    Love,
                    Rachel

7.
a. isn't
b. couldn't
c. they're
d. she'll

8.
a. The log floated (on) the water.
b. She sat (on) the chair.
c. The bird flew (over) the roof.

9.
a. I danced and sang.
b. The boy laughed and played.
c. The dog ran and barked.

10.

(Date) February 10, 1991

(Greeting or Salutation) Dear Grandma,

(Body)
Mom and Dad gave me a puppy for my birthday. He is so cute. I named him Rascal. Please come and see my new puppy.

(Closing) Love,

(Signature) Rachel

The Poetry Unit

Skills

Titles of poems, songs, etc.
Titles of books, ships, etc.
Underlining
Quotation marks
Rhyme
Couplet
Cinquain   Diamante   Limerick

"America the Beautiful"

O beautiful for spacious skies,
For amber waves of grain,
For purple mountain majesties
Above the fruited plain!

America! America!
God shed His grace on thee
And crown thy good with brotherhood
From sea to shining sea!

"America the Beautiful" by Katherine Lee Bates (1859-1929)

Teacher's Note: As your student completes each lesson, choose skills from the Review Activities that he needs. The Review Activities follow each lesson.

1.

b. *spacious* skies
amber waves of grain
shining sea

1. a. Listen while your teacher reads the poem aloud. Read the verses silently while your teacher reads it aloud a second time. As your teacher reads, listen to the descriptions and try to imagine the settings described.

b. Look over the poem and use the dictionary to look up any words you don't know. Write sentences using these words. Adjectives (describing words) are words that help paint pictures. They tell more about a noun or pronoun. Find the adjectives that describe these nouns in our literature passage and underline them:

skies   waves of grain   sea

c. List four to six words that you should study for spelling this week, or use the following list of suggested words: beautiful, spacious, skies, majesties.

In Lesson 6, you learned how to form the plural with words ending in **y**. Before you add an **s** to words ending in **y**, look at the word. If the word ends with a vowel and **y**, just add **s**. If the word ends with a consonant and **y**, change the **y** to **i** and add **es**.

> **Spelling Tip**
> To form the plural with words ending in a consonant and **y**, change the **y** to **i** and add **es**. To form the plural with words ending in a vowel and **y**, just add **s**.

d. Complete the chart.

vowel and y   **consonant and y**

1) monkey
2) key
3) pulley
4) alley
5) toy
6) majesty
7) sky
8) puppy
9) pony
10) entry
11) penny

2. a. Punctuation helps us understand what words and phrases
   mean. They also help us read correctly. For example, a
   sentence that ends with an exclamation point is read with
   strong emotion. A period tells you to come to a complete
   stop.

   b. Since you have heard the poem read, learned the meaning
   of the words, and studied the punctuation, you are
   now ready to begin reading the poem with expression.
   Practice reading the poem as if you were presenting it
   for others. Speak slowly and clearly, with a voice loud
   enough to be easily heard. You may want to tape record
   yourself so that you can make improvements. Begin
   memorizing the poem as well.

3. a. Write the title of the poem.
   When you write the title of a song, poem, or story,
   capitalize the first word and every other important word.
   Enclose the title with quotation marks.

   b. Write the following titles correctly:
   1) the three little pigs (story)
   2) how great thou art (song)
   3) roses are red (poem)

1.
d.   vowel and y
   1)   monkeys
   2)   keys
   3)   pulleys
   4)   alleys
   5)   toys

        consonant and y
   6)   majesties
   7)   skies
   8)   puppies
   9)   ponies
   10) entries
   11) pennies

3.
a. "America the Beautiful"

b. 1) "The Three Little
       Pigs"
   2) "How Great Thou
       Art"
   3) "Roses are Red"

3.

d. 1) Little House in the Big Woods *or Little House in the Big Woods*

  2) Trumpet of the Swan *or Trumpet of the Swan*

  3) Farmer Boy *or Farmer Boy*

  4) Addie Saves the Day *or Addie Saves the Day*

  5) The Escape of the Slave Trader *or The Escape of the Slave Trader*

  6) National Geographic *or National Geographic*

  7) Old Ironsides *or Old Ironsides*

f. Answers will vary.

g. Answers will vary.

c. Titles of books, movies, magazines, and ships are also capitalized the same way. But instead of using quotation marks, the title is underlined.

   Note: If computer generated, use italics instead of underline.

d. Write the following titles correctly:
   1) little house in the big woods (book)
   2) trumpet of the swan (book)
   3) farmer boy (book)
   4) addie saves the day (book)
   5) the escape of the slave trader (book)
   6) national geographic (magazine)
   7) old ironsides (ship)

e. The title "America the Beautiful" is a good description of our country. Either by looking through magazines, newspapers, catalogs, travel brochures, or your family's own photographs, choose four pictures that show some part of "America the Beautiful." Mount or glue the pictures on construction paper. (Ask your teacher for permission before cutting them out.)

f. In **1b** of this lesson, we looked at the adjectives the author used in our literature passage to describe America. Make a list of three or four words that describe each picture you have chosen. For example, looking at a picture of a mountain sunset, one might use these adjectives to describe it: *colorful, grand, peaceful, or beautiful.*

g. Write one or two sentences that describe each picture using the adjectives on your list on the bottom or back of the construction paper.

h. Review your spelling words.

4. a. Listen as your teacher reads the passage about "America the Beautiful" from *Color the Patriotic Classics.* You may want to color the picture of the 1893 Chicago World's Fair, attended by the woman who wrote "America the Beautiful," Katharine Lee Bates, found on page 151 of the *Student Activity Book.*

America the Beautiful
Katharine Lee Bates
1859-1929

Katharine Lee Bates was born August 12, 1859, in Falmouth, Massachusetts. As the daughter of a pastor, she was raised during a time in history when studying God's Word was more important than math or science. She knew her Scriptures well because she spent much of her youth memorizing them. As a young girl she developed an extensive vocabulary. While other children were outside playing, Katharine, who loved the English language, chose to stay inside to read her books.

It was the summer of 1893, school was out and there would be no more English classes for three months. Katharine and a group of other teachers traveled to Colorado to see the expanding West. Along the way, they attended the World's Fair in Chicago.

The World's Fair of 1893 was known as The White City for its white lights and white buildings. The ten-million dollar fair was more than anyone could have ever imagined. Countries from around the world were invited to participate. The lagoons and canals of Venice were replicated on six square-miles of swampy land. It was so huge that people did not know where to start or where to go.

After the exposition in Chicago, Katharine and her group went to Pike's Peak in Colorado. She saw deep purple mountains against a turquoise sky, fields of grain, and immense open plains. She said, "It was there, as I was looking out over the sea-like expanse of fertile country spreading away so far under ample skies, that the opening lines of this text formed themselves in my mind.

Later that evening, she and her fellow teachers discussed the trip through Chicago, the mountain climbing, and the breath-taking view they had just experienced. The whole sleepy group retired for the evening, except for Katharine, who could not fall asleep. She took a pencil and paper and found herself writing about the events of the day in poetic form. The words naturally formed themselves into *C.M.D.**

As she remembered the mountains she thought of Isaiah:

"How beautiful upon the mountains are the feet
of him that bringeth good tidings of peace."

The memorization of Scripture as a child helped her to construe:

"O beautiful for pilgrim feet,
Whose stem impassioned stress,
A thoroughfare for freedom beat
Across the wilderness!"

She completed the poem and placed it in her notebook. Six years later, in 1899, she found the poem, rewrote the text to simplify it and sent it to a publisher in Boston. The hymn was printed in the *Congregationalist*. Katharine received many letters suggesting she put her words to music. She asked composers to send in tunes. She received sixty tunes but not one fit the words. Later, in 1926, the "National Federation of Music Clubs" held a contest to set the poem to a new tune. Nine hundred entries were sent. None were acceptable and no prize was awarded. The tune we sing today is known as Materna. A New Jersey businessman named Samuel Ward, wrote the tune 10 years before Katharine's text. No one knows how Ward's tune and Bates' poem were coupled but it is the only version we sing today.

* C.M.D: Common Meter Doubled. A hymn where first and third lines are 8 syllables each and second and fourth lines are 6 syllables each. The pattern is then repeated.

Used by permission from *Color the Patriotic Classics*. One in the series of historical books and musical cassette tapes from *Color the Classics* by Carmen Ziarkowski.

b. Optional: Review your spelling words.

Used by permission from *Color the Patriotic Classics*. One in the series of historical books and musical cassette tapes from *Color the Classics* by Carmen Ziarkowski.

5.

a. It sounds like the author is expressing appreciation for the abundance of America. They sound like a prayer.

b. 8, 6, 8, 6, 8, 6, 8, 6.

c. grain, plain, thee, sea

 Teacher's Note: There is an internal rhyme of *good* and *brotherhood*.

5. a. Our literature passage contains eight lines, with two parts containing four lines each. Read the first four lines and tell your teacher what you think the author is telling you about America. What do the last four lines sound like to you?

b. The poem, "America the Beautiful" follows a pattern. Count the number of syllables in each line, then tell your teacher the syllable pattern of the verse.

c. Notice which words rhyme. Point them out to your teacher.

d. Try to make up a four sentence poem that follows this pattern of 8 syllables, 6 syllables, 8 syllables and 6 syllables, with the last word in the 2nd and 4th lines rhyming. You may use the sentences you wrote in **3g**, or make up new sentences. Illustrate your poem with your own drawings or another picture cut out of a magazine. Ex:

> I'd like to climb this tree today.
> It is so very tall.
> I'll watch my step and hold on tight.
> So I won't slip and fall.

e. Present "America the Beautiful" to your family or class by reading or reciting from memory. You may also want to present the poem you wrote.

f. Optional: Take a spelling test.

g. Optional: Choose skills from the *Review Activities* on the next page.

Review Activities

Choose the skills your student needs to review.

1. *Titles of Books, Movies, Ships, Magazines, etc.*
   Capitalize and underline.

   a. the last battle (book)
   b. the secret garden (book)
   c. chariots of fire (movie)
   d. time (magazine)

2. *Titles of Songs, Poems, Stories, etc.*
   Capitalize and add punctuation.

   a. mary had a little lamb (poem)
   b. how great thou art (song)
   c. who has seen the wind? (poem)
   d. all things bright and beautiful (poem)
   e. silent night (song)

1.
a. <u>The Last Battle</u> or *The Last Battle*
b. <u>The Secret Garden</u> or *The Secret Garden*
c. <u>Chariots of Fire</u> or *Chariots of Fire*
d. <u>Time</u> or *Time*

2.
a. "Mary had a Little Lamb"
b. "How Great Thou Art"
c. "Who has Seen the Wind?"
d. "All Things Bright and Beautiful"
e. "Silent Night"

Teacher's Note: If a poetry book is available, find other couplets to read aloud to your student.

1.

b Lines 1 and 2

c. Possible answers:
   1) hair
   2) me
   3) mat, hat

Pattern Poetry

1. a. Read the following poem aloud to your teacher.

      Eenie meenie minie mo
      Catch a tiger by its toe.

      If he hollers let him go
      Eenie meenie minie mo.

   b. Which lines rhyme?

   c. In poetry, two lines that rhyme is called a **couplet**.

      Complete the following couplets.

         1) I saw a brown bear
            He was covered with _____ .
         2) I saw a little bee
            He looked straight at _____ .
         3) I saw a black cat
            He sat on the _____ .

   d. Try writing two or three couplets on your own.

   e. Read your couplets aloud.

2. a. Listen to your teacher as she reads the following poem.

      Spider
      Many hands
      Weaves and spins
      Web of golden threads
      Masterpiece

   b. Now, read the poem aloud to your teacher.

c. This kind of poetry is called a **cinquain**. A cinquain contains five lines which follow a pattern. Try writing a cinquain following the directions below.
Line 1 - Write a one word topic.
Line 2 - Write two words describing the topic.
Line 3 - Write three words telling the action of the topic.
Line 4 - Write four to five words expressing you feeling.
Line 5 - Write the same word as in Line 1, or a synonym, or another related word.

d. Read your cinquain aloud.

3. a. Listen to your teacher as she reads the following poem.

Shower
W e t , c o l d
Raining, watering, cleansing
Children sigh, children play
Shining, Singing, Smiling
Bright, Colorful
Rainbow

b. Now, read the poem aloud to your teacher.

c. What shape does the poem look like?

This poem is called a **diamante** because the poetry lines form the shape of a diamond.

d. Follow the directions below and write your own diamante.

Line 1 - Write a one word topic. (Line 7 will be an antonym for this word.)
Line 2 - Write two words describing the topic.
Line 3 - Write three words describing the actions of the topic.
Line 4 - Write two words relating to the topic in Line 1; and two words relating to the word in Line 7.
Line 5 - Write three words describing the actions of the word in Line 7.
Line 6 - Write two words describing the word in Line 7.
Line 7 - Write an antonym for the topic word in Line 1.

e. Read your diamante aloud.

Teacher's Note: If a poetry book is available, find other cinquains to read to your student.

Teacher's Note: This is a word cinquain. There is also a syllable cinquain.

Teacher's Note: If a poetry book is available, find other diamantes and read them to your student.

3.
c. A diamond

✏ **Teacher's Note:** If a poetry book is available, find other limericks to read to your student. When reading the limerick aloud to your student, be sure to stress your voice when you see the stress marks ('́).

4. a. Listen to your teacher as she reads the following poem.

There wás a young lády, whose nóse
Continually próspers and gróws
When it gréw out of sight
She exclaimed in a fright
"Oh! Farewéll to the end of my nóse!"

b. Now, read the poem aloud to your teacher. The stress marks ('́) show you where to emphasize your voice.

c. This kind of poetry is called a **limerick**. A limerick is a humorous poem of five lines. Try writing your own limerick following the directions below.

Line 1 - three stressed syllables
Line 2 - three stressed syllables;   Lines 1, 2, and 5 rhyme
Line 3 - four stressed syllables;   Lines 3 and 4 rhyme
Line 4 - four stressed syllables
Line 5 - three stressed syllables

d. Read your limerick aloud.

5. a. If a poetry book is available, read some poems on your own.

b. Which pattern poetry did you enjoy the most? Spend today writing any pattern poetry of your choice: couplet, cinquain, diamante, or limerick.

c You may want to illustrate any of the poems you have written this week.

I C.A.N. Assessment

for

Poetry Unit

After the *Unit* is completed, check off
each **I** C.A.N. objective with your teacher.

C ____ I can **complete** my work.

____ I can be **creative**.

A ____ I can be **accurate**.

____ I can do my work with a good **attitude**.

N ____ I can do my work **neatly**.

EVERYDAY WORDS

in

David Livingstone, Foe of Darkness

Skills	
Antecedent	Quotations
Compound Words	Research
Plurals	Suffix
Prefix	Synonym

Altogether different was the reception given him a week later by an important chief. **This native was enchanted to see a white man and very curious to know what brought him to a section where only traders had ever come.** *David told him of his mission, and the chief begged to learn about the white man's God.*

Text excerpt, pg. 52 from *David Livingstone, Foe of Darkness*, by Jeannette Eaton. Copyright © 1947 by William Morrow and Company, Inc. By permission of William Morrow and Company, Inc.

1. a. Read the literature passage silently. Ask your teacher to help you with difficult words. When you are ready, read the passage out loud to your teacher. In your own words, tell your teacher what is happening in this passage.

   b. As your teacher reads the lines in bold print out loud, write them down. Compare your copy to the literature passage and make corrections.

   c. List four to six words that you should study for spelling this week, or use the following list of suggested words: native, curious, brought, section.

Spelling Tip
Some words with the short /o/ sound, like *bought* are spelled with **ough**.

Copy these words, and underline **ough**. Say the words aloud as you write them.

brought	wrought
fought	ought
sought	bought

2. a. Look at the first sentence of the literature passage. The last word is *chief*. To form the plural of words ending in **f** or **fe**, say the plural word aloud. If you hear the **/f/** sound, just add **s**.
Ex: chief - First, say the singular word. Then say the plural word. You can still hear the **/f/** sound, so spell it *chiefs*.

Now say the plural for *wife*. The **/f/** sound has changed to a **/v/** sound. Therefore, change the **f** to **v** and add **es**.
Ex: wife - wives

b. Write the plural form of the following words. Say the plural word aloud. Do you hear the **/f/** or **/v/**?
1) knife
2) roof
3) loaf
4) hoof
5) life
6) belief

Note: Do not confuse the plural noun *beliefs* with the verb believe.

c. Look at the last sentence of the literature passage. It refers to the *white man's God*. Do you remember why the apostrophe is used in *man's*?

d. To form the plural possessive form, usually just add the apostrophe (') after the plural form.
Ex: trader's village - singular possessive
      traders' village - plural possessive

Write the plural possessive form for the following words.
1) carpenter's tools
2) coach's plans
3) candidate's speeches
4) tree's roots
5) car's shine

2.
b. 1) knives
   2) roofs
   3) loaves
   4) hooves
   5) lives
   6) beliefs

c. The apostrophe shows ownership.

d. 1) carpenters' tools
   2) coaches' plans
   3) candidates' speeches
   4) trees' roots
   5) cars' shine

2.

e. 1) men's mission
   2) women's clothing
   3) children's room
   4) teeth's enamel
   5) mice's bottle

✐ **Teacher's Note: Gus'
book and Jesus's robe are
also acceptable.**

3.

a. the work to preach the
gospel.

b. recep<u>tion</u>, sec<u>tion</u>,
mi<u>ssion</u>

---

e. To form the plural possessive form of irregular words,
usually just add the apostrophe and **s** (**'s**).
Ex: child's mother - singular possessive
children's mother - possessive

Write the plural possessive form for the following
irregular words.
1) man's mission
2) woman's clothing
3) child's room
4) tooth's enamel
5) mouse's bottle

f. To form the plural possessive of singular one-syllable
words ending in **s**, usually add an apostrophe (**'**) and **s**.
Ex: Gus's book

g. To form the plural possessive of singular words of two or
more syllables ending in **s**, usually just add an apostrophe (**'**).
Ex: Jesus' robe

3. a. David Livingstone's upbringing and education influenced
him to decide to become a doctor. He wanted to be a
doctor so he could go into unexplored areas and do the
work of a missionary. Look up the word *missionary* in
the dictionary. Tell your teacher what a missionary is, and
what he tries to do. The word *missionary* has the word
mission as its base. Look up the word *mission* and write a
definition for it that relates to the work of the church.

b. There are three words in our literature passage that end
with the sound **/shun/**. Find them and write them in a
list. There are four letters at the end of each word that
spell the sound **/shun/**. Underline these last four letters
in each word on your list.

> ### Spelling Tip
> Words ending with the **/shun/**
> sound are usually
> spelled with **-tion** or **-sion.**

c. What are the two ways to spell this sound?

c. tion, sion

d. Read the following list of words to your teacher. Notice that each word ends with the **/shun/** sound. Though some of these words may be long, the syllables in these words are easy to hear. Try to spell these words orally for your teacher after she reads each one to you. If this is difficult, ask your teacher to read them slowly, emphasizing each syllable. Try to use these words in a writing assignment so you will become more comfortable writing and reading them.

information	vacation	division	invasion
civilization	definition	tension	decision

e. Review your spelling words.

4. a. **Research** is the process of looking for information in books like encyclopedias, dictionaries, or resource books. Normally, we research a particular subject.

   Do research to try to locate some basic information about David Livingstone. Look for information about his life and work in Africa. Encyclopedias have information on him, as do books about him or his African explorations. If a library is available to you, go there and use the card catalog (either an actual card catalog or computer) to locate resources on David Livingstone. Find two or three of these books with your teacher's help.

   b. There are some basic facts about David Livingstone's life that can be determined by answering the following questions. Answer these questions in writing. Use complete sentences.
   1) Why did Dr. Livingstone go to Africa?
   2) When did Dr. Livingstone go to Africa?
   3) What were his most important discoveries?
   4) What famous meeting occurred between Dr. Livingstone and another man?
   5) How do you think Dr. Livingstone would want to be remembered?

4.
b. 1) as a medical missionary
   2) 1840
   3) Victoria Falls, Zambia River, and lake Nyalsa; he crossed the continent
   4) Henry Stanley asked, "Dr. Livingstone, I presume?"
   5) preaching, teaching and healing.

145

4.

c. Possible answers:
David Livingstone
came to Africa as a
medical missionary in
1840. He discovered
Victoria Falls, and was
the first man to explore
the Zambezi River and
Lake Nyasa. He also
was the first to cross
the continent of Africa.
Henry Stanley was sent
to find Livingstone,
who people thought
was dead. When
they met, he said,
"Dr. Livingstone, I
presume?" Though he
made many famous
discoveries, his first
love was preaching,
teaching and helping
the sick

c. You may use the answers to the questions in **4b** to write a paragraph about David Livingstone. Write a sentence that tells what the paragraph is about. This will be your **topic sentence**. Then make up at least three sentences that tell details about Livingstone's life. These are called **supporting sentences**. Remember to **indent** the first sentence by beginning about five spaces from the left margin.

d. Optional: Take an oral or written spelling pretest.

5. a. Listen as your teacher reads the literature passage for dictation. Do not write as it is read the first time, just listen. Remember, writing from dictation is a skill you acquire with practice, like hitting a baseball. Your first attempts may not be too successful, but as you practice you will become better.

b. After you listen to the literature passage the second time, write what you have heard. When you have finished, compare your copy to the literature passage.

c. Optional: Take a spelling test.

d. Optional: Choose skills from the *Review Activities* on the next page.

Review Activities

Choose the skills your student needs to review.

1. *Plurals*
   Write the plural form for the following words.

   a. wife
   b. roof
   c. loaf
   d. hoof
   e. knife

2. *Plural Possessive Nouns*
   Write the plural possessive form for the following phrases.

   a. the room belonging to the kids
   b. the toys belonging to the girls
   c. the office belonging to the men
   d. the playroom belonging to the children

3. *Research*

   a. What are some resources you can use when doing research?
   b. What is a topic sentence?
   c. What are supporting sentences?

1.
a. wives
b. roofs
c. loaves
d. hooves
e. knives

2.
a. kids' room
b. girls' toys
c. men's office
d. children's playroom

3.
a. encyclopedia, dictionary, library, computer, etc.
b. the main sentence which tells what the paragraph is about
c. sentences in a paragraph which support the topic sentence

One afternoon David sat with him under a great baobab tree. The chief was full of praise for the English doctor's skill in curing a young tribesman of a badly infected wound.

Then suddenly the chief flung out both his hands in passionate entreaty. "I wish you would change my heart. Give me medicine to change it, for it is proud and angry, angry always."

Text excerpt, pg. 52 from *David Livingstone, Foe of Darkness*, by Jeannette Eaton. Copyright © 1947 by William Morrow and Company, Inc. By permission of William Morrow and Company, Inc.

1. a. Read the literature passage silently. Ask your teacher to help you with difficult words. When you are ready, read the passage out loud to your teacher. Narrate to your teacher what is happening in this passage.

   b. As your teacher reads the lines in bold print out loud, write them down. Compare your copy to the literature passage and make corrections.

   c. List four to six words that you should study for spelling this week, or use the following list of suggested words: curing, wound, doctor, praise.

   Spelling words with the /ow/ sound can be tricky. Some words are spelled **ow** and some are spelled **ou**. Although there is no rule to tell you which /ow/ to use, remember that **ou** will usually not end a word.

> **Spelling Tip**
> Words are spelled with **ou** or **ow** to make the */ow/* sound, but **ou** will usually not end a word.

d. Copy these words, and underline **ow** and **on.** Say the words aloud as you write them.

ow	**ou**
down	wound
cow	snout
growl	cloud
plow	flounder
owl	mountain

2. a. Look at the first sentence of the literature passage. Can you find a word which is made up of two words joined together? This is called a **compound word**.

   b. Find the other compound word in the next sentence.

   c. Match the words from the columns to make compound words.
   1) dog   man
   2) sun   sit
   3) flash   house
   4) mail   rise
   5) baby   light

   d. Look at the last paragraph of the literature passage. List all the personal pronouns. Beside each pronoun, write the noun for which it refers. You may refer to the Pronoun Chart on page 12.
   Ex: One afternoon David sat with him under a great baobab tree. him - the chief

   The word which the pronoun refers to is called the **antecedent**.

3. a. In the second paragraph of our literature passage, the chief asks David for medicine to change his heart. Tell your teacher why do you think he asks David for this medicine? Reread the first part of the passage for a clue to the answer.

   b. Why does the chief want his heart to be changed? What is he trying to change?

2.
a. afternoon

b. tribesman

c. 1) doghouse
2) sunrise
3) flashlight
4) mailman
5) babysit

d. his-chief; I-chief
you-David; my-chief;
me-chief; it-heart;
it-heart.

3.
a. The chief saw David
use medicine to heal a
tribesman.

b. His heart is proud and
angry, and these are
feelings he wants to be
gone from his heart.

3.

c. The chief seems desperate. He greatly desires to be free from his angry spirit.

4.

a.

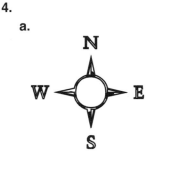

b.

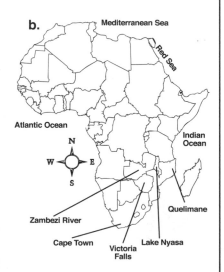

c. Refer to map above.

c. How does the chief seem to feel about what he is saying to David? There are two words that give us clues - *passionate entreaty*. Look up these two words in the dictionary and tell your teacher how you think the chief feels.

d. Review your spelling words.

4. a. Look at a map of Africa in your atlas or on the next page. Find the **compass** and point it out to your teacher. This is a common item on most maps.

   There are two main types of maps:
   political (includes divisions for countries)
   physical (shows land formations like mountains)

   You will need an atlas, almanac, or other book with a detailed map of Africa as a reference. In pencil write the following locations on your map of Africa.

   Atlantic Ocean   Red Sea
   Mediterranean Sea   Indian Ocean

   b. Locate Cape Town on your map. Place a dot there and label it. Locate these other places of interest of Dr. Livingstone's explorations:

   Victoria Falls   Lake Nyasa (also known as Lake Malawi)
   Zambezi River

   c. Livingstone is also known as the first white man to cross Africa. He began in Cape Town and took four years to reach Quelimane, which was a Portuguese settlement on the east coast of Africa. Try to find Quelimane on a map of Africa, and label it on your map.

   d. Add as many of these main features to your map as you can: The Nile River and the present-day names of countries. If the countries on your map are too small, you can write the names on the ocean area with a line pointing to the country.

   e. Optional: Take an oral or written spelling pretest.

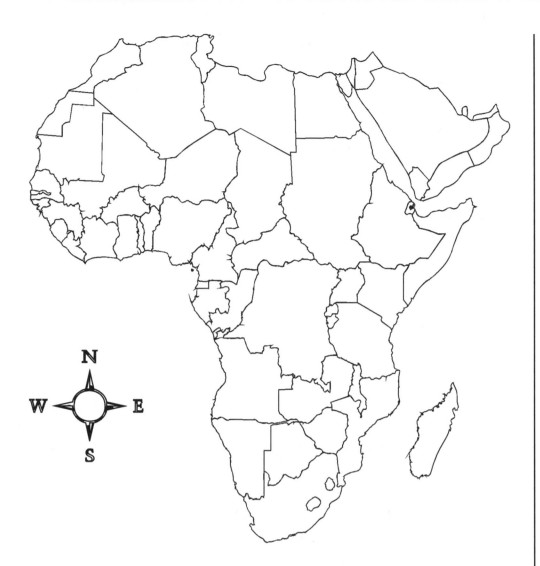

5. a. Listen as your teacher reads the literature passage for
dictation. Do not write as it is read the first time, just
listen. Remember, writing from dictation is a skill you
acquire with practice, like hitting a baseball. Your first
attempts may not be too successful, but as you practice
you will become better.

b. After you listen to the literature passage the second time,
write what you have heard. When you have finished,
compare your copy to the literature passage.

c. Take a spelling test.

d. Optional: Choose skills from the *Review Activities* on the
next page.

Review Activities

Choose the skills your student needs to review.

1. *Compound Words*
   Make compound words using the following words.

   a. fish   hook
   b. bird   beat
   c. book   life
   d. wild   seed
   e. heart   store

2. *Antecedent*
   Underline the pronoun, and circle the antecedent for each pronoun.

   a. Sam fed his snake.
   b. The snake crawled in its cage.
   c. Sam and Russell traded their cards.
   d. After trading cards, they ate lunch.
   e. "Would you like to go swimming?" asked Sam.
   f. "I would love it," said Russell.
   g. "Let's go after we finish our lunch," said Sam.

1.
a. fishhook
b. birdseed
c. bookstore
d. wildlife
e. heartbeat

2.
a. his, Sam
b. its, snake
c. their, Sam and Russell
d. they, Sam and Russell
e. you, Russell
f. I, Russell
g. we, our, Sam and Russell's

Looking into the glowing dark eyes, David said gently, "If you will let the loving spirit of Christ enter your heart, it will be changed."

"Nay!" cried the chief and beat his breast with both hands. "I wish to have it changed by medicine and to have it changed at once, for it is always very proud and very uneasy and continually angry with someone."

Text excerpt, pg. 52 from ***David Livingstone, Foe of Darkness***, by Jeannette Eaton. Copyright © 1947 by William Morrow and Company, Inc.

1. a. Read the literature passage silently. Ask your teacher to help you with difficult words. When you are ready, read the passage out loud to your teacher. In your own words, tell your teacher what is happening in this passage.

   b. As your teacher reads the lines in bold print out loud, write them down. Compare your copy to the literature passage and make corrections.

   c. List four to six words that you should study for spelling this week, or use the following list of suggested words: heart, changed, spirit, chief.

   If you get confused about **ie** or **ei**, just remember that if the word makes a long /**e**/ sound, it will usually be spelled **ie**, except when it comes after **c** like *receive*. If the word makes a long /**a**/ sound, it will also be spelled **ei**.

   > ### Spelling Tip
   > i before e except after c and
   > in words that say /ay/
   > like neighbor and weigh.

   Copy the words, and underline **ie** and **ei**. Say the words aloud as you read them.

i before e -	chief	friend	niece
cei -	receive	ceiling	receipt
ei /ay/ -	neighbor	weigh	veil

2.

a. "If you will let the loving spirit of Christ enter your heart, it will be changed."

b. "Nay!" "I wish to have it changed by medicine and to have it changed at once, for it is always very proud and very uneasy and continually angry with someone."

c. Punctuation marks are usually included inside the closing quotation marks.

3.

a. Uneasy; -un means not.

b. unhappy
unpaid
unlike

c. Unhappy - not happy
Unpaid - not paid
Unlike - not like

2. a. Today, we will review quotations. Find the exact words that were spoken by David Livingstone and underline them with a red pencil or pen.

b. A new paragraph begins when a new person speaks. Using a blue pencil or pen, underline the exact words spoken by the chief. His words are divided into two sentences, so be sure to mark only the words he said.

c. Look at both underlined passages. Find the punctuation marks at the end of each sentence. Are they inside the quotation marks, or outside?

d. With permission, listen to a conversation or dialogue between two people, and try to write down three or four sentences from their discussion. (The best way to get all the words both people speak is to tape record the conversation, with their permission, of course.) As you write down the conversation, you will need to add speech tags such as *Mom said,* or *Bill asked.* If you just write down what they said, it will be difficult to understand who is speaking. Remember to place quotation marks where they are needed.

3. a. In the last sentence of our literature passage the word *easy* has been used, with a prefix added to it. Find this word. What is the prefix and what do you think it means?

b. Prefixes are added to the front of base words, and they change the meanings of the words. Look at this picture of a house that demonstrates adding prefixes and suffixes.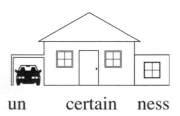

un   certain   ness

Rewrite these words adding the prefix **un-** to each one.

happy   paid   like

c. Tell your teacher how you think the prefix **un-** changes the meanings of these words.

d. Rewrite these sentences using a word with the prefix **un-** attached to it:
1) The road is not even.
2) I am not certain about the weather.
3) The chair was not comfortable.

e. Make up three more sentences using a word that includes the prefix **un-**. Look in the dictionary under **un-** if you are having trouble thinking of words.

f. Review your spelling words.

4. a. Reread the literature passages from Lesson 18, 19, and 20 to your teacher. Although the chief wants medicine to cure his angry heart, what does David tell the chief he must do to cure his heart?

b. Discuss with your teacher the message that David Livingstone told the chief.

c. What response does the chief give David?

d. Does the chief accept David's advice?

e. Why not?

f. Discuss with your teacher the emotions behind David's words in this week's literature passage. Which word tells you how David spoke to the chief?

   Say the exact words David spoke, with the tone of voice you think he used.

g. Say the words of the chief, with the tone of voice you think he used. You may act out the chief's words if you would like.

h. Optional: Take an oral or written spelling pretest.

d. 1) The road is *uneven*.
   2) I am *uncertain* about the weather.
   3) The chair was *uncomfortable*.

e. Answers will vary.

4.
a. David told the chief that he must "let the loving spirit of Christ" enter his heart.

b. Allow for discussion.

c. The chief's response is "Nay!"

d. He does not accept David's advice.

e. He prefers to have medicine change his heart so that his heart will be changed immediately.

f. David spoke his words *gently*.

5. a. Listen as your teacher reads the literature passage for dictation. Do not write as it is read the first time, just listen. Remember, writing from dictation is a skill you acquire with practice, like hitting a baseball. Your first attempts may not be too successful, but as you practice you will become better.

    b. After you listen to the literature passage the second time, write what you have heard. When you have finished, compare your copy to the literature passage.

    c. Optional: Take a spelling test.

    d. Optional: Choose skills from the *Review Activities* on the next page.

Review Activities

Choose the skills your student needs to review.

1. *Quotations*
   Rewrite the following dialogue adding capitalization and punctuation.

   a. what has hands but has no feet asked mary
   b. I don't know said leo
   c. a clock has hands but has no feet said mary

2. *Prefix **un-***
   Add the prefix **un-** to the following words.

   a. do
   b. cover
   c. available
   d. tie
   e. safe
   f. selfish
   g. believable

3. What does the prefix **un-** mean?

1.
a. "What has hands but has no feet?" asked Mary.
b. "I don't know," said Leo.
c. "A clock has hands but has no feet," said Mary.

✏ Teacher's Note: Be sure the student indents for each new person speaking.

2.
a. undo
b. uncover
c. unavailable
d. untie
e. unsafe
f. unselfish
g. unbelievable

3. not

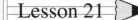

Teacher's Note: As your student completes each lesson, choose skills from the Review Activities that he needs. The Review Activities follow each lesson.

David smiled pityingly at this very human wish for a quick dose of holiness. "Alas, medicine heals only the body. Love, a thing of the spirit, must push anger from your heart."

Text excerpt, pg. 52 from *David Livingstone, Foe of Darkness*, by Jeannette Eaton. Copyright © 1947 by William Morrow and Company, Inc. By permission of William Morrow and Company, Inc.

1. a. Read the literature passage silently. Ask your teacher to help you with difficult words. When you are ready, read the passage out loud to your teacher. In your own words, tell your teacher what is happening in this passage.

   b. As your teacher reads the lines in bold print out loud, write them down. Compare your copy to the literature passage and make corrections.

   c. List four to six words that you should study for spelling this week, or use the following list of suggested words: pityingly, holiness, medicine, heart.

   Before you add the suffix **-ness** to a word ending in **y**, look the word. If the word ends with a consonant and **y**, change the **y** to **i** and add **-ness**.

   > ### Spelling Tip
   > When adding **-ness** to words ending in a consonant and **y**, change the **y** to **i** and add **-ness**.

1.
d. happiness
    loveliness
    emptiness
    laziness

   d. Complete the chart. Say the words aloud as you write them.

   -ness

Ex:	holy	holiness
	happy	
	lovely	
	empty	
	lazy	

Teacher's Note: The word pitying does not drop the y because the suffix begins with a vowel.

   Bonus Question: Look at the word *pityingly* in our passage and tell your teacher why the **y** was left on the end of *pity* when we added suffixes to it.

2. a. Suffixes are endings we add to words to change their meanings. We start with a base word, and then add a suffix. Here is a picture:

   In this lesson, find the word with the base word *holy* with a suffix added to it. Be careful, because the spelling of the word *holy* was changed to add the suffix. Circle the word.

   kind   ness

   b. The suffix **-ness** means *the state of being*. Read the following sentence. What do you think the word *kindness* means?
   Ex: We all noticed her *kindness*.

   c. Write a sentence with each of the words you made in **1d**.

   d. Look at the second sentence of the literature passage. What part of speech do you think *Alas* is?

   e. Rewrite the sentence separating *Alas* and *medicine* with an exclamation mark. Watch your capitalization.

   f. Write these words taken from the literature passage. Beside each word, write a word of opposite meaning. This is called an **antonym**.
   Ex: happy - sad
   1) smiled
   2) quick
   3) heals
   4) love
   5) push
   6) anger

3. a. Review the definitions we have previously learned about adverbs. They tell us how, when, where, or how much something was done. Adverbs often end with the letters **-ly**. The words *very*, *so*, and *really* are usually adverbs because they tell how much there is of something. Underline the adverbs in the literature passage with a red pencil.

2.
a. holiness

b. The state of being kind.

c. Possible answers:
We wish the bride and groom much *happiness*.
I was awed by the *loveliness* of the painting.
Ron felt an *emptiness* in his heart.
Laziness rots the bones.

d. Interjection

e. "Alas! Medicine heals only the body."

f. Possible Answers:
1) frowned
2) slow
3) hurts
4) hate
5) pull
6) love

3.
a. pityingly, very

3.

b. Answers will vary.

c. Answers will vary.

4.

a. David was very compassionate and understanding of the chief's feelings.

b. Jeanette Eaton, the author of *David Livingstone, Foe of Darkness*, uses a dramatic style in her writing. Her use of adverbs and adjectives helps us to understand her meaning. Look over the four passages from Lessons 18-21 and choose three sentences that you think are descriptive and well written. Copy them below leaving a blank line between each sentence.

c. Using colored pencils, underline the adjectives in red. Try to think of a synonym (word close to the same meaning) for each adjective. Write a synonym above each adverb. If you need help, you can use a dictionary or thesaurus.

Next, underline the adverbs in blue. Try to find a synonym for each adverb if you can. Write a synonym above each adverb. Read the sentence or phrase using the synonyms. Remember these adjectives, adverbs, and synonyms when you write. Try to use at least one new word each week either in your writing or speaking.

d. Review your spelling words.

4. a. David Livingstone said of himself, "I am a missionary, heart, and soul." He is well-known for all of his explorations and discoveries in Africa, but he also said that this was not what was most important to him. In the literature passage, we see a missionary's heart towards those he talks with. Describe David's attitude toward the chief.

b. If you know any missionaries personally, ask them if you may have an interview. Ask them to tell you about their goals, travels, and know their lives have been different from other families. Ask them what they have done that they feel has helped people. If you do not know any missionaries personally, perhaps you have family members or friends who can tell you about missionaries they have known.

c. There have been many famous missionaries who have traveled to different parts of the world to tell people about the Gospel. If you would like, you can study a missionary in greater detail. Using library books, look for stories about missionaries. Choose one missionary, read about him, and then tell your class about his life. Here are some suggestions if you can't think of one:

> Eric Liddell (missionary to China)
> Amy Carmichael (missionary to India)
> Billy Graham (evangelist to the world)
> Apostle Paul (missionary to Greece, Rome)

d. Optional: Take an oral or written spelling pretest.

5. a. Listen as your teacher reads the literature passage for dictation. Do not write as it is read the first time, just listen. Remember, writing from dictation is a skill you acquire with practice, like hitting a baseball. Your first attempts may not be too successful, but as you practice you will become better.

b. After you listen to the literature passage the second time, write what you have heard. When you have finished, compare your copy to the literature passage.

c. Optional: Take a spelling test.

d. Optional: Choose skills from the *Review Activities* on the next page.

Review Activities

Choose the skills your student needs to review.

1. *Suffix **-ness***
   Add the suffix **-ness** to the following words.

   a. gentle
   b. happy
   c. kind
   d. wining
   e. clever
   f. lonely
   g. ill

2. What does the suffix **-ness** mean?

3. *Antonyms*
   Write antonyms for the following words.

   a. laugh
   b. break
   c. clean
   d. frown
   e. awake
   f. deep

4. *Synonyms*
   Write synonyms for the following words.

   a. kind
   b. run
   c. sleepy
   d. skinny
   e. want

1.
a. gentleness
b. happiness
c. kindness
d. willingness
e. cleverness
f. loneliness
g. illness

2. state of being

3. a. cry
    b. fix
    c. dirty
    d. smile
    e. asleep
    f. shallow

4.
a. generous, unselfish, nice
b. hurry, jog, sprint
c. drowsy, dreamy
d. scrawny, thin, slight, lean
e. desire, crave

Assessment 4
(Lessons 18 - 21)

1. Write the following nouns in its plural form.

   a. loaf
   b. knife
   c. roof

2. Write the following plural nouns in its possessive form.

   a. the toys belong to the children
   b. the cards belonging to the boys
   c. the cars belonging to the men

3. Make compound words using the following words.

   a. mouse   spoon
   b. door   trap
   c. snow   knob
   d. tea   man

4. Underline the pronoun and circle the antecedent for each pronoun.

   a. Robert fixed his bike.
   b. Mom made her famous apple pie.
   c. Tim and Jake talked with their friend.

5. Look at this word: unhappy

   a. What is the base or root word?
   b. What is the prefix?

6. Look at this word: illness

   a. What is the base or root word?
   b. What is the suffix?

7. What are some resources you can use when doing a research?

---

1. a. loaves
   b. knives
   c. roofs

2. a. children's toys
   b. boys' cards
   c. men's cars

3. a. mousetrap
   b. doorknob
   c. snowman
   d. teaspoon

4.
a. (Robert) fixed his bike.
b. (Mom) made her famous apple pie.
c. (Tim and Jake) talked with their friend.

5.
a. happy
b. un

6.
a. ill
b. ness

7. encyclopedia, computer, library books, videos, etc.

8. possible answers
  a. sick
  b. smooth
  c. pull

9. possible answers
  a. clever
  b. skinny
  c. courageous

10.
  a. meat - A dog eats meat.
  b. flower - I can smell a flower.
  c. blue - I like the color blue.

8. Write antonyms for these words:

   a. healthy
   b. rough
   c. push

9. Write synonyms for these words:

   a. smart
   b. thin
   c. brave

10. Write homonyms for these words:

   a. meet - I will *meet* you at noon.
   b. flour - Mom needs *flour* to bake bread.
   c. blew - The wind *blew* through the trees.

Oral Presentation

and

Folk Tales

CHORAL READING

1. In Lesson 8 you spent a week preparing a read-aloud presentation. Talk to your teacher about that experience. What did you enjoy about it? What did you not like about it?

   This week, you will work with one or more people to prepare a choral reading presentation. This type of presentation can feel more comfortable because you have others standing with you before the audience. Preparation is still very important.

   The first step is to choose the others who will read with you. You may include your teacher, too. You may use as many people as you wish, but no more than four is suggested for one week of preparation.

   Secondly, determine your audience and the type of material they will enjoy hearing. Since you are working with other readers, you may choose a longer piece than you used last time.

2. Meet with all the readers, and read over your chosen material to learn the meaning of it. Talk to your teacher about words you do not understand. Try to find out what the author wanted to communicate.

   Read the material again looking for the emotion (feelings) behind the words. Did the author want us to laugh, cry, learn, etc. when we read this work? Talk to your teacher about how you might use your voice to express these feelings. Ask these questions:

   1) What will we emphasize as we speak?
   2) Where will we pause as we speak?
   3) Will we use our voices in any other manner to communicate the meaning?

If you will be presenting a story, your group may need to use different kinds of voices for each character. Ask these questions:

1) What do we need to emphasize?
2) Where do we need to pause?
3) How do we need to use our voices to communicate the meaning?

In choral readings you must decide which lines will be read by whom and which lines will be read by everyone. Many times the lines that need emphasis are read by everyone.

Look at the following psalm and read it aloud as directed. That will help you get the feel of choral reading. The example is given for four readers. You may adapt it to the number of students.

If you have 2 readers:
    Person 1 - reads 1 and 3
    Person 2 - reads 2 and 4

If you have 3 readers:
    Person 1 - reads 1 and 4's - He guides me ...
    Person 2 - reads 2 and 4's - Thy rod...
    Person 3 - reads 3 and 4's - Surely, goodness...

Psalm 23

ALL:	The Lord is my shepherd, I shall not want.
Person 1:	He makes me lie down in green pastures;
Person 2:	He leads me beside quiet waters.
Person 3:	He restores my soul;
Person 4:	He guides me in the paths of righteousness
ALL:	For His name's sake.
Person 1:	Even though I walk through the valley of the shadow of death,
Person 2:	I fear no evil;
Person 3:	For Thou art with me;
Person 4:	Thy rod and Thy staff, they comfort me.

Person 1:   Thou dost prepare a table before me in the presence of my enemies;
Person 2:   Thou has anointed my head with oil;
Person 3:   My cup overflows.
Person 4:   Surely (*pause*) goodness and loving kindness will follow me all the days of my life,
ALL: And I will dwell in the house of the Lord forever.

Assign parts for the material you have chosen to present. You may want to copy the material for each reader and let each reader mark his part.

3 and 4. Practice reading your material aloud at least three times each day. You are not required to memorize the entire passage; however, you should know it well enough to be able to look up from your book several times during the presentation.

Stand in front of a mirror as you practice. Use the following list to help you evaluate yourself. After you have practiced several times, ask your teacher or another student to evaluate you, using the list.

Oral Presentation Checklist
1. Do we read slowly?
2. Do we read clearly?
3. Do we read loud enough?
4. Are we using our voices well to communicate the meaning and feeling?
5. Are we standing up straight, but naturally?
6. Do we look at our audience enough?

Decide how all the readers will stand as they present their reading. You may form a pattern, depending on the height of the readers.

Ex: Taller Readers

Audience

Be sure the audience can see everyone and everyone can see the audience. Taller readers should be in the back while shorter readers should be in front. The readers may hold scripts in their hands, or a large print of the reading can be held up in the back of the room.

5. Your presentation day has arrived, and even though you may feel nervous, you are ready for your audience because you planned for it. If you feel very nervous, ask your teacher to sit in the back of the room and give you support by smiling at you.

1. a. Listen as your teacher reads the story of "The Mission of John Chapman," or read it silently to yourself. This story is called a **folk tale** or **legend**.

The Mission of John Chapman
Retold by Linda Fowler

On the day baby Chapman was born, at a time when our nation was still mostly wilderness, people remarked that the sky seemed especially blue. The air was fresh and crisp, the fields were teeming with wildflowers, and the sweet smell of apple blossoms, carried along by a gentle breeze, floated into every nook and cranny of each little cabin in the village. Truly, spring had come to Massachusetts, and everyone declared it a perfectly wonderful day to be born. But nobody—not even his mama or papa—could have imagined the great mission that lay ahead for that tiny little bundle they named John.

Johnny grew quickly (as children are apt to do), and very early on it became clear that this young fellow looked at the world just a little differently than most others his age. As a toddler—mind you, a TODDLER—he'd content himself for hours sitting in the yard, chattering with the birds as he coaxed them to take seeds and berries right out of his hand. Later, instead of romping with children from the village, he much preferred to frolic with furry little wild things that lived in the woods and fields around his home.

Now obviously, since woodland creatures were his favorite friends, Johnny absolutely refused to take up hunting when he came of age—and that, as you probably know, was completely unheard of for a farm boy at that time. As a matter of fact, folks had a pretty hard time finding anything about Johnny that they considered normal. Still, as odd as he seemed, no one ever found fault with his strong faith (his parents were careful to see that he knew the Gospel) or his kind, peaceful nature.

It was well-known that a person could depend on young John Chapman to pitch in whenever he needed help doing something. He often amazed neighbors with his knowledge of the medicines and remedies that could be made from different plants. But more important than all that was the cheerful way he went about doing those boring day-to-day chores most everybody else hated.

One thing he didn't enjoy, though, was school! It seemed perfectly silly to Johnny to spend good daylight hours stuck inside a cramped, stuffy little building. So, even though he attended (out of respect for his parents' wishes), each day of confinement produced more and more imaginary trips into the outdoors—which is where he really wanted to be, after all.

Of course, this bothered his teacher who, first of all, didn't think daydreaming was a good thing to do in school and second, was convinced that "dreamers" could only turn into unproductive adults. He was a very practical man.

Johnny though, for his part, was perfectly content with his formal education once he learned to read well enough to understand the Bible. He already knew more about animals and plants than most adults, and he had a knack for speaking the truth in simple ways. As he grew older, he took to reading large sections of Scripture out loud to his animal friends who, strangely, seemed to listen. Again, pretty odd behavior for a boy–but it was about this time that he became convinced God had a special task waiting for him...just around the corner.

The spring he turned 18 began like any other, except that for Johnny there was a strange excitement in the air–a sense of adventure so real he could almost touch it. The thought popped in his head that maybe, just maybe, it was time to strike out on his own and find his calling, that thing, whatever it was, he was so certain God wanted him to do.

Naturally, when he brought the idea to his parents it took them a few minutes to settle down, because deep inside, they'd always hoped Johnny would be content to marry and raise his family close to home.

But on the other hand, they weren't really surprised either. They knew their son well, that he'd always been happiest wandering through woods or wading in streams. Besides, it seemed that nowadays the roads and rivers carried a steady trickle of wagons and boats westward. The fact was, hundreds of reasonable people had become "dreamers," leaving everything familiar behind and traveling bravely to unknown places and new beginnings.

So they agreed–but only if Johnny would take along his brother, Nathaniel, as a traveling companion. They hoped that Nat, since he was only 11, might keep "home" in Johnny's mind so he wouldn't want to stray too far. Well, that seemed like a fine idea to Johnny, and Nat, as you might have guessed, liked it even better.

Now it happened that Uncle Ben Chapman lived in western New York, in a town named Olean, and his farm seemed as good a destination as any. So very early one morning, the boys stuffed a couple of gunny sacks with such things as a Bible, a few clothes and some food, slung the bags over their shoulders, and set out on the greatest adventure of their young lives.

They walked a very, very long time to get to Olean, but neither of the boys minded because there were so many new and wonderful things to see. At night, they often shared campfires and news with other travellers, but during the day they mostly chose to enjoy the peace of the wilderness by themselves.

One day, as they rested under a huge oak that grew beside an apple orchard, the brothers watched something unusual happen on the trail they'd been traveling. A large wagon stopped almost directly in front of them, and a family piled out. The children though, instead of frolicking through the green field, walked solemnly to the edge of the orchard–uttering not one word–and stood staring at the trees (which were still pink with sweet-smelling blossoms). Their mama and papa stood silently, also gazing toward the orchard, till the woman turned slightly, buried her face in her husband's shoulder and wept quietly.

As quickly as it began, the little drama ended. No one ever noticed John and Nat watching from under the oak as the children were called back to their places and the family resumed its journey. But Johnny pondered the scene for weeks after. From that moment on, he became increasingly aware of the fact that, in the wilderness areas they travelled, there were NO fruit trees. There were acres and acres of fir, oak and beech trees, and some berry bushes here and there–but fruit trees appeared only in areas that had been settled for years and years. And of course, the further they walked, the further apart these settlements were.

Naturally, noticing this made Johnny remember special times at home. He thought about the heavenly scent of apple blossoms in the spring, and the crisp, sweet crunch of fresh apples in the fall. He remembered his mama stringing apples up in the kitchen to dry, so there'd be applesauce all winter, and he could almost taste the mouth-watering pies and sweet cider she made. Right then and there, Johnny decided that apples were indeed a very special gift from the Lord, and now it saddened him to think about all the hard-working, brave folks headed west with no friendly apple trees to look forward to.

At any rate, when the Chapman boys finally reached Olean they were in for a surprise. Their Uncle Ben's cabin sat empty and deserted, and word was he had packed up the year before to head for a settlement called Marietta, in Ohio. Now, believe it or not, both Johnny and Nathaniel were completely tickled to hear this news because neither boy was ready to give up the fun of exploring quite yet.

Since it was too late in the summer to start another long journey on foot, Johnny decided to look for work there in Olean. And guess what he found? Why, a job helping a farmer with his apple orchard, of course! He couldn't have been happier, and he learned a great deal in a very short time from the kindly man.

That autumn, at harvest time, Johnny drove a wagon loaded with apples to the cider mill, and it was there that God's plan for his life began to take shape for the first time. You see, as he watched the mill slowly grind the apples and press out their juice, his eyes suddenly rested on the small mountains of squeezed pulp that littered the millyard. Why, he had never seen so many seeds in one place at one time—and it dawned on him that each and every one was actually an apple tree, just waiting for a chance to grow!

He thought back to the pioneer family he'd watched say a sad goodbye to the joys of apples before they headed west; he considered his great love of wandering and the outdoors; he looked again at the thousands of seeds, and all at once his mission in life lay before him as clearly as anything he'd ever seen before.

So it began—the kindest, gentlest, most selfless legend our country ever produced started right there in that millyard, as Johnny Chapman knelt to the task of sorting, washing, and drying apple seeds. He continued this tedious work throughout the long winter, and by spring had several good sized sacks ready to go as he and Nat set out for Ohio.

On this journey, the boys were forced to travel lighter than before because of all those seeds! No extra clothes went with them this time, and food stores were limited to a sack of corn meal (they'd become quite fond of pone). Of course, Johnny's Bible rested inside his shirt, and he took to wearing the cooking pot on his head, like a hat, since that seemed like a logical place to carry the thing. Along the way, he handed out packets of seeds and favorite Scriptures to every frontier-bound family they met, and he carefully planted a few of the precious seeds in each clearing they passed.

You can see that by the time he took leave of Nathaniel at Uncle Ben's in Marietta, his pattern was well set. And, naturally, several large orchards began to sprout in the rich, black earth around the Ohio River soon after he tramped on into the wilderness beyond.

John fulfilled his mission for over 50 years, pushing further and further west, but always returning to the Ohio River basin to tend his orchards there before beginning his circuit again. It's said that when his clothes and shoes wore out, he took to wearing a rough sack with holes cut for his head and arms, and going barefoot. The pot on his head became a trademark, and his favorite traveling companion turned out to be a big, black wolf he'd once rescued from a trap.

But as odd a character as he continued to be, this man was truly beloved by all, and everyone watched for his appearances. He preached the Gospel to settlers, Indians and animals alike, and spread God's apple-blessing as far west as his legs would carry him. Yet few actually knew his name. To almost everyone he was always just Johnny Appleseed.

b. Think about Johnny's life divided into three time periods:

1. Childhood and Youth (up to 18 years old)
2. Young Explorer (explorations with Nathaniel)
3. On His Own (after he left Uncle Ben's)

c. Skim: Look over the story to remember the main ideas of each paragraph. It is not necessary to read every word. **Skimming** is a quick reminder of what you have read. To skim a story you have not read before, read titles and probably the first sentence of each paragraph. This will give you an idea of what the story is about.

d. Scan: Go back again, and now look for specific events that go into each of the three time periods mentioned in **1b** above. By **scanning**, make a list of three events from each part of Johnny's life that was the most interesting or exciting.

2. a. Take a piece of paper and fold into thirds.

On the top part, write the heading *Childhood and Youth*. On the middle part write the heading *Young Explorer*, and on the bottom part write the heading *On His Own*.

Using the lists you developed yesterday, make up a sentence to describe each event. Write each sentence in the correct section on your divided paper.

b. When you are finished, you will have written three groups of sentences about John Chapman. Read each group of sentences aloud to your teacher and talk about any changes you could make to improve the wording.

c. Using the heading for each section, make up a sentence that tells about that part of Johnny's life. These sentences will be your **topic sentences** for each paragraph. Here's an example:
Childhood and Youth—Johnny Chapman had an unusual childhood and youth.

Talk with your teacher and write a sentence for each section on your paper. These are called **supporting sentences**.

3. a. Today, you will learn to write a **summary** report. Think about the main points or most important things about the story.

   b. Begin the first paragraph, or **introduction**, by including the following information:

   - Who is the story about?
   - When did the story take place?
   - Where did the story take place?

   c. The second paragraph will tell what the story is about. Write this paragraph by including the following information:

   - What are the main events in the story?

   d. The last paragraph will be the **conclusion**. Include the following information:

   - What do you think about Johnny Chapman?
   - Did you like the story? Why?

4. a. You have now completed a summary report on the story "The Mission of John Chapman." Try to think of a title for your report that tells about what you have written. Ask your teacher to look over your paragraphs and help you find any mistakes in punctuation or spelling. This is called **proofreading**.

   b. After corrections have been made, rewrite or type your report into its final form. This should include your name and date in the upper right hand comer.

3.
a. **Possible Introduction: The title of the story is "The Mission of John Chapman." The story is about a young boy and how he grew up. The story takes plalce in Massachusetts during the wilderness days.**

d, **Possible conclusion: I liked Johnny Chapman because he was kind and helped people and animals. I also liked the story because it shows how one person can do a great thing.**

5.

a. Possible answers:
   peaceful, kind,
   faithful, dependable,
   cheerful, imaginative,
   adventurous, selfless,
   gentle

5. a. You have read about and discussed the life of John Chapman. Today you will write a few sentences that tell about Johnny Chapman. This is called a **character sketch**. Find page 204 of the *Student Activity Book* or using a piece of blank paper, write *Johnny Chapman* in the middle and draw a circle around it. Now scan your story for specific adjectives, or words, that describe Johnny. Write these words in the circle as shown here. After you have finished, draw circles around each word, and attach them to the big circle with a line.

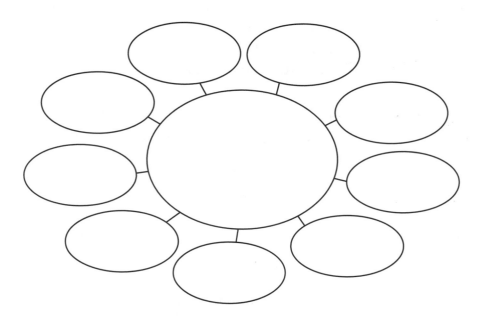

b. Read over what you have written. Talk with your teacher and see if you can think of any more words not included in the story that you think describe Johnny. Add these words to your character sketch. Now write sentences about Johnny Chapman using your character sketch.

c. Using the same approach, make a character sketch that describes you. Write your name in the middle with a circle around it. Talk with your teacher and come up with a list of adjectives, or descriptions that tell about you. Try to be honest, but always be kind. Write these words around the main circle and draw circles around each word and attach them with a line to the big circle.

Take this opportunity to talk with your teacher about your strengths and weaknesses. You may want to set goals for improving some area of your life, or you may want to start thinking of ways that you can better use your strengths.

d. Optional: Choose skills from the *Review Activities* on the next page.

✎ **Teacher's Note:** In approximately six weeks, your student will begin lessons on the book *Amos Fortune, Free Man.* In preparation, we suggest you assist your student in ordering original source documents to accompany the study.

A booklet of original documents such as Amos' will, receipts, photos, articles, etc. may be ordered for $10.00 plus $2.00 shipping. Make checks payable to Town of Jaffrey and allow 4-6 weeks for delivery.

Order from:
Director of
Jaffrey Public Library
38 Main Street
Jaffrey, NH 03452

1. Answers will vary.

Review Activities

1. Write a summary of the short story, "Paul Bunyan and the Whistlin' River," found on page 77.

BOOK STUDY

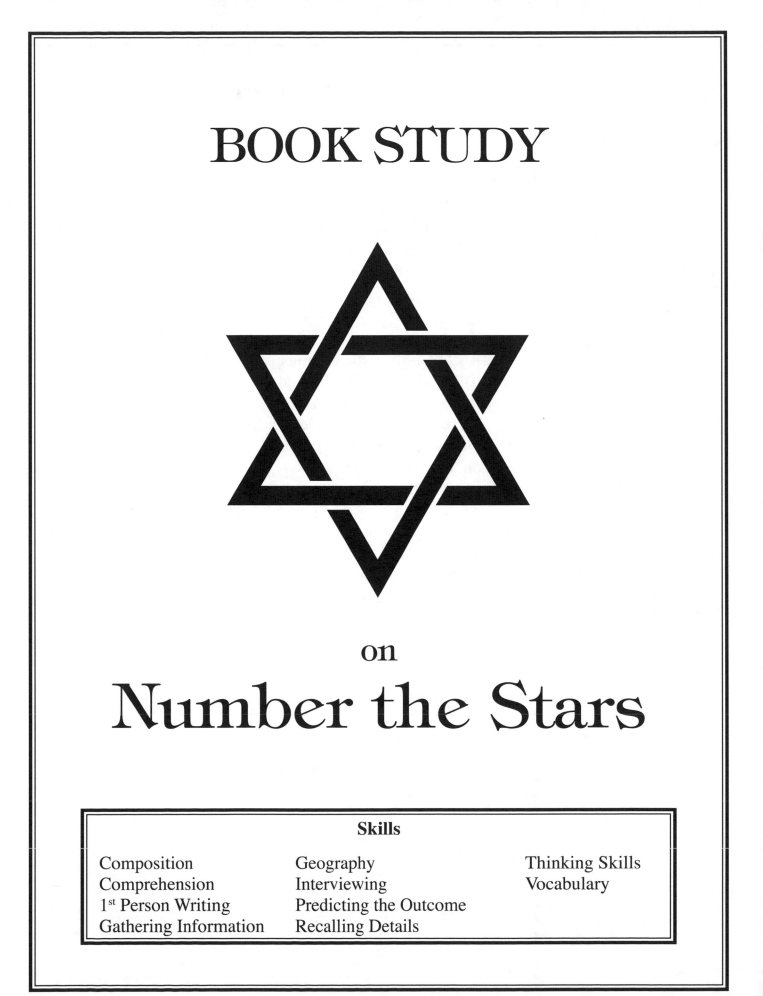

on
Number the Stars

Skills		
Composition	Geography	Thinking Skills
Comprehension	Interviewing	Vocabulary
1st Person Writing	Predicting the Outcome	
Gathering Information	Recalling Details	

Number the Stars
by Lois Lowry
Copyright 1989
Houghton Mifflin Harcourt
Publishing

✐ **Teacher's Note:**
This story is a gentle introduction to World War II and the Holocaust. While the story includes the disappearance of Jewish families, there is no mention of the horrors of their camps. In chapter 16, a fisherman calls the Nazi dogs "damn dogs" because they are able to locate people hiding in the boats. If you desire to scratch the word out of the book your student is reading, that will not affect the story. We believe the story is so well presented; we do not want one word to keep it out of our program.

Introducing
Number the Stars

Spark:
Find a map of Europe or use the one in the *Purple Student Activity Book*. Show your student Denmark. Discuss its size in relationship to the nearby countries. Point out Sweden and discuss its location in relationship to Denmark.

Summary

In 1943, during the German occupation of Denmark, a ten year old and her family learned to be brave and courageous when they helped shelter a Jewish family from the Nazis. On every street corner in Denmark stood two Nazi soldiers to monitor and control the people. One day, a Jewish lady's button store was closed and a sign on the door indicated the Nazi government closed the store. It became clear that the Jewish families were being relocated in Denmark. Annemarie Johansen and her family risked all to help their Jewish friends escape to Sweden where they can be safe. Along the way, Annemarie learned about trust and bravery.

Vocabulary

Find the following words in context. Read the sentences before and after the word. What do you think the word means? Look up the word online or in a dictionary and write the meaning that best suits its context in this story.

1. rucksack (Chapter 1)

2. obstinate (Chapter 1)

3. café (Chapter 1)

4. halt (Chapter 1)

5. resistance (Chapter 3)

6. swastika (Chapter 3)

Use the correct vocabulary word in to complete each sentence.

OR

Write your own sentences with the words.

1. We met at the _____ for a sandwich.

2. The German officer had a _____on his uniform.

3. He carried all his books in a _____.

4. Many brave people worked in the _____ Movement in Europe.

5. The soldier shouted, "_____," and we stopped immediately.

6. Kirsti could be an _____ child.

1. rucksack – a type of backpack

2. obstinate - firmly adhering to one's purpose, opinion

3. café – a small restaurant usually with an outdoor section

4. halt – stop, cease moving

5. resistance – the act of opposing a force

6 swastika – A figure used as a symbol or an ornament since prehistoric times. This figure was the official emblem of the Nazi party and the Third Reich

1. café

2. swastika

3. rucksack

4. Resistance

5. halt

6. obstinate

1. The girls were afraid of the soldiers because they had guns and were so big and powerful.

2. Mama told the girls to walk another way because she did not want the soldiers to know their faces.

3. Denmark surrendered because they did not have an army and King Christian X knew Denmark could not win a battle.

4. The King had all the Danish ships burned so the Nazis could not use them.

5. Mrs. Hirsch's shop was closed and had a sign on it. Mrs. Hirsch was Jewish.

6. Annemarie is afraid something will happen to her Jewish friend, Ellen.

7. The Germans controlled the importing of goods.

8. It was hard to find shoes. The people could not get coffee or sugar.

Discussion Questions

Find the section of the book that answers these questions. Be prepared to read the sections to your teacher or group.

Chapter 1

1. Explain why the girls were afraid of the soldiers.

2. Why did Mama tell the girls to walk another way to school?

Chapter 2

3. Explain why the King of Denmark surrendered to Germany.

4. What did the Danish do to their ships after the Nazis took over Denmark? Why?

Chapter 3

5. What was unusual about Mrs. Hirsch's shop?

6. Why was Annemarie frightened that evening?

Chapter 4

7. Why do you think it was so hard for the people to buy things in Denmark?

8. What things were they not able to buy?

Chapter 5

9. Why was Ellen staying with Annemarie's family?

10. Who awakened them during the night?

11. How did Papa 'save the day'?

Chapter 6

12. Where did Mama and the girls go for vacation?

13. Describe Uncle Henrik and his life.

Chapter 7

14. What was across the sea from Uncle Henrik's town?

15. Why did Annemarie hide Ellen's necklace?

Chapter 8

16. Why did Mama prepare the living room?

9. The Rabbi told the people that they would be relocated soon. The Rosens were making plans to escape.

10. Soldiers knocked on the door and wanted to know the location of the Rosen family. The soldiers questioned that the girls were sisters since one had dark hair.

11. Papa pulled out a photo of Lise and Annemarie when they were young and Lise has dark hair, convincing the soldiers.

12. Mama and the girls went to Uncle Henrik's house.

13. Uncle Henrik was a fisherman who lived alone.

14. Across the sea from Uncle Henrik's town was Sweden. It was free of Nazi rule.

15. Annemarie hid Ellen's necklace because it was a Star of David and would prove that Ellen was Jewish.

16. They were going to put a casket in the room.

17. Annemarie did not know of a Great-aunt Birte and had not heard of anyone in the family who had died.

18. Uncle Henrik told her that it was easier on some people if they did not know the truth, and then they would not have to lie if they were questioned.

19. Annemarie did not want Ellen to have the burden of the truth if she were asked.

20. The soldiers came to the house because they saw many people coming there.

21. When the soldier wanted to open the casket, Mama told him that the person died of typhus and may still be contagious.

22. In the casket were blankets and jackets.

23. Peter was there to help the Jewish families escape.

24. Mama took the Rosens to Uncle Henrik's boat so he could take them to Sweden where they would be free.

25. Annemarie found a packet that Peter had given Mr. Rosen. Peter said it was very important.

Chapter 9

17. Why did Annemarie think that Mama and Uncle Henrik were lying to her?

18. How did Uncle Henrik explain the lies to Annemarie?

19. Why did Annemarie not tell Ellen the truth about Great-aunt Birte?

Chapter 10

20. Why did the soldiers come to the house?

21. How did Mama 'save the day'?

Chapter 11

22. What was in the casket?

23. Why was Peter there too?

Chapter 12

24. Where was Mama taking the Rosens? Why?

Chapter 13

25. What did Annemarie find at the bottom of the steps?

Chapter 14

26. Where was Annemarie going that took her through the woods?

27. What was at the end of the path?

Chapter 15

28. How did Annemarie decide to act with the soldiers?

29. What happened when the soldier found the special packet?

Chapter 16

30. How did Annemarie show her bravery?

31. Why was the handkerchief so important?

Afterword

32. What parts of this story are true?

26. Annemarie took the packet to Uncle Henrik's boat.

27. When she came to the end of the path she saw Nazi soldiers and their dogs.

28. Annemarie decided to act like Kirsti, her younger sister.

29. When the soldier found the packet, he opened it and saw only a handkerchief.

30. Annemarie was afraid to go through the woods and face the soldiers, but she did to save her friends.

31. The handkerchief had a powder on it that would attract the dogs but then make their sense of smell non existent. That prevented the dogs from finding people on the boats.

32. The surrender of Denmark to the Nazis and the reason for it is true. The bombing of the ships was factual. The escape of Jewish families to Sweden was true. The powder on the handkerchief was true and used to help Jewish families escape Denmark.

Story Activities

1. Locate Denmark on the map of Europe. Color it red. Find Sweden and color it green. Draw a line showing the route taken by Jewish families who escaped to Sweden.

2. Go online or find a book that shows the countries that were taken over by the Nazis in the 1930s and 1940s. Color all of these red.

3. Interview people who know about World War II. Write a paragraph or two about the information you obtain.

4. Choose one of the main characters from the story: Mama, Annemarie, Ellen, Peter, and Uncle Henrik.

   Choose a section of the story and write it from that character's point of view.

5. Think about bravery and what it means to you. Write a short story about a character who acts bravely in a difficult situation. You may use a story you heard in your interviews.

I C.A.N. Assessment

for

Number the Stars - Book Study C

After the *Book Study* is completed, check off each **I C.A.N.** objective with your teacher.

C ___ I can **complete** my work.

___ I can be **creative**.

A ___ I can be **accurate**.

___ I can do my work with a good **attitude**.

N ___ I can do my work **neatly**.

EVERYDAY WORDS

in
Strawberry Girl

Skills	
Outline	Syllables
Compound Subject	Compound Verb
Simile	Descriptive Verb
Verb tense	Directions

Listen as your teacher reads "The History of Strawberry Girl" found below.

The History of Strawberry Girl
by Wanda Fisher

Connecticut Yankee Lois Lenski did not grow up dreaming of becoming a writer. She wanted to draw. She spent hours copying photographs and magazine covers, while her father indulged her budding creativity with a new box of water colors.

Later the secret world of books began to entice her. Kate Douglas Wiggin, Louisa May Alcott, and Frances Burnett were her mentors. Still, the tug of the world of art captured her fancy.

She was a practical woman, too, being taught at a young age that work was good and excellence was a goal to strive for. She took design courses at college and learned how to draw a house plan, how to hand-letter, and how to draw cartoons. But what she loved most was drawing children.

Everywhere she went, she carried a sketch book -- and a note book. She was a meticulous, dutiful journalist, capturing moods on faces and emotions in words. Instead of picturing herself as merely an illustrator of other peoples' ideas, friends encouraged her to come up with her own stories. It was good advice.

Her lifelong habit of studying people led her to first develop only books on children of the past. She was an avid researcher; however, she soon tired of knowing people only second-hand. She wanted to write about real life and real people. After making several trips to the South, she began to realize just how diverse America was.

She came up with the idea of a series of regional books, exploring how children lived in different parts of the country. Her second regional book was *Strawberry Girl*. Lois Lenski wanted to accurately portray the world of the Florida "Cracker," and she carried out her research in a very unobtrusive way. To do research for *Strawberry Girl*, she traveled with a County Health nurse who was doing a survey of her maternity patients north of Lakeland. Lois would accompany her and store her impressions of the people -- how they spoke, dressed, lived -- and record them when alone.

Mrs. Lenski soon discovered that the world of the Florida strawberry farmer relied on three things to insure success -- the soil, the mild Central Florida winter, and... Mr. Henry Plant. The first strawberry plants in Florida may have been set as early as 1881, when settlers from Mississippi (seeking a milder climate) were astounded at the rich dark top-soil around Polk County, that was said to be six feet deep! These delicate plants could be set out in the fall, and could begin being harvested as early as January. Soon, the strawberry's fame began to spread and neighbors were trading runners with each other, and a new industry was birthed.

But success led to other problems. Soon, so many strawberries were being grown, that a way had to be found to transport them to other markets quickly. The problem was solved, however, by the farsightedness of industrialist Henry B. Plant, another Connecticut Yankee, whose Central Florida railroad line connected the east and west coast of Florida. Tampa boomed; and the delicate fruit of the strawberry could now be picked, sold for cash at Farmer's Markets, and be transported (packed in ice) to excited buyers in the North. Strawberry growing was at first a family business since they required hand labor and farms could easily be managed by one family. The "Strawberry School" was soon developed, since it would close and allow students to harvest the fruit during the months of January, February, and March. If frost threatened, the whole family would work together to cover the delicate plants with straw.

This was the world of the Boyers that Lois Lenski captured for us in *Strawberry Girl*, which won her a Newbery Award in 1946. It was a rural, bound-to-the-earth existence, yet rich in love. It was that world that captured Mrs. Lenski and persuaded her to spend her latter years in her "adopted" homeland, Florida.

1. Talk with your teacher about the main points of the history.
    a. Who was Lois Lenski?
    b. What is the story of *Strawberry Girl*?
    c. How did the growing of strawberries become a success in Florida?

2. a. An outline is an organized way of preparing your writing. Look at the sample outline below.

    ```
    I. Main Point

       A. Detail or Example #1
       B. Detail or Example #2

    II. Main Point

       A. Detail or Example #1
       B. Detail or Example #2

    III. Main Point

       A. Detail or Example #1
       B. Detail or Example #2
    ```

1.
a. Lois Lenski, from Connecticut, authored several regional books including *Strawberry Girl*.
b. *Strawberry Girl* is a story about life in early Florida, or the Florida "Cracker."
c. The rich soil and the mild Florida climate allowed strawberries to be harvested in January.

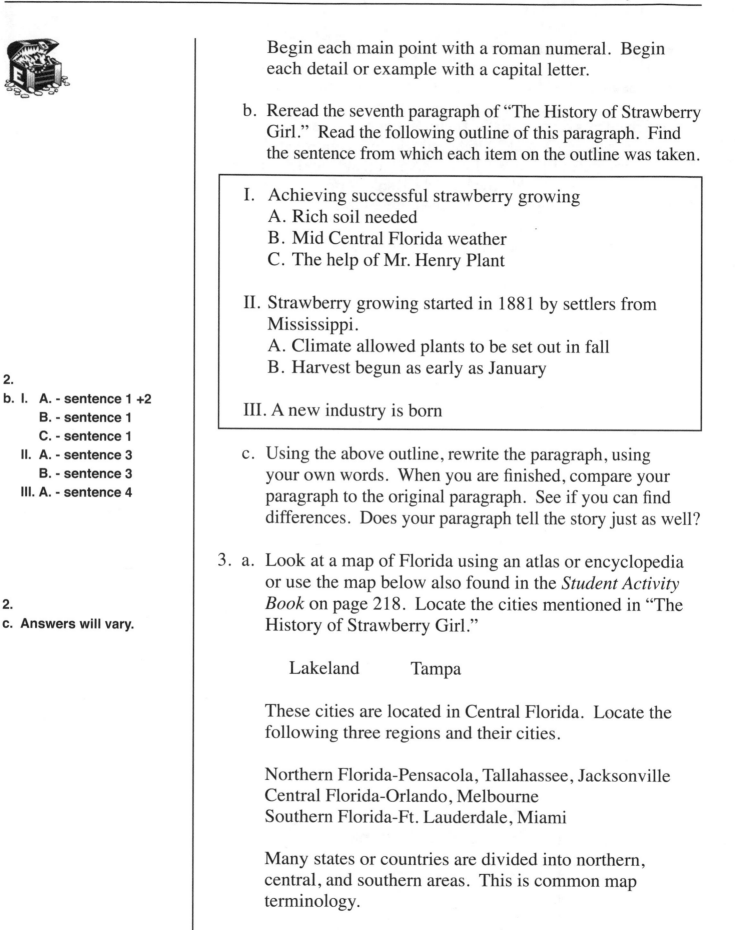

Begin each main point with a roman numeral. Begin each detail or example with a capital letter.

b. Reread the seventh paragraph of "The History of Strawberry Girl." Read the following outline of this paragraph. Find the sentence from which each item on the outline was taken.

I. Achieving successful strawberry growing
   A. Rich soil needed
   B. Mid Central Florida weather
   C. The help of Mr. Henry Plant

II. Strawberry growing started in 1881 by settlers from Mississippi.
   A. Climate allowed plants to be set out in fall
   B. Harvest begun as early as January

III. A new industry is born

2.
b. I. A. - sentence 1 +2
   B. - sentence 1
   C. - sentence 1
  II. A. - sentence 3
   B. - sentence 3
  III. A. - sentence 4

c. Using the above outline, rewrite the paragraph, using your own words. When you are finished, compare your paragraph to the original paragraph. See if you can find differences. Does your paragraph tell the story just as well?

2.
c. Answers will vary.

3. a. Look at a map of Florida using an atlas or encyclopedia or use the map below also found in the *Student Activity Book* on page 218. Locate the cities mentioned in "The History of Strawberry Girl."

    Lakeland   Tampa

These cities are located in Central Florida. Locate the following three regions and their cities.

Northern Florida-Pensacola, Tallahassee, Jacksonville
Central Florida-Orlando, Melbourne
Southern Florida-Ft. Lauderdale, Miami

Many states or countries are divided into northern, central, and southern areas. This is common map terminology.

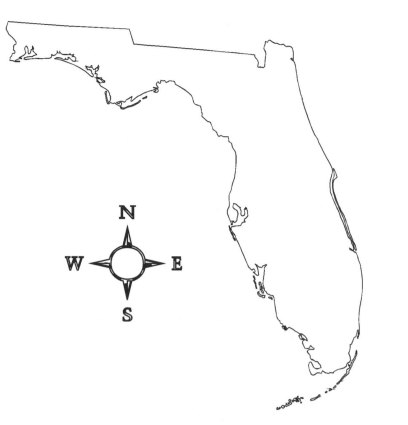

3. a.

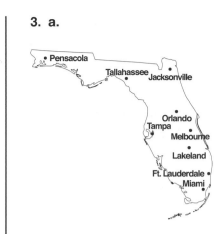

b. Look at a map of your state and find the northern, central, and southern sections. Identify one city in each region. (If you live in Florida, you may want to get a map of your city and find a street in the northern, central, and southern parts of your city.)

c. Look at a map of the continental United States (excluding Alaska and Hawaii). The United States is usually thought of more in terms of eastern, central and western states. Find states that would be considered a part of each classification: eastern, central, and western. For more complex identification, two directions can be combined. Looking at the compass on the map, find these directions:

    northeast   northwest
    southeast   southwest

Find a state that you think would fall into each directional category: northeast, northwest, southeast, and southwest.

4. a. Reread the eighth paragraph of "The History of Strawberry Girl," found on page 188. Talk to your teacher about the two main points of the paragraph. On a sheet of paper, copy the following outline, or use the outline found in the *Student Activity Book.*

4.
a. Possible Answers:
I. Problems
  A. too many
    strawberries
  B. transportation
II. Solution
  A. Henry B. Plant
  B. railroad
III. etc,

I.
  A.
  B.
II.
  A.
  B.

Using phrases (not complete sentences), write the first main point of the paragraph next to roman numeral one (**I**). Write the second main point next to roman numeral two (**II**).

Reread the paragraph, looking for at least two details about each main point. Write the details next to the letters **A** and **B** in your outline.

b. Give your outline to your teacher. Ask your teacher to tell you what the paragraph is about, using only your outline. Was your teacher able to discover the main points of the paragraph from your outline? Discuss this with your teacher, and change any points in your outline, if necessary.

5. a. Using the outline you wrote yesterday, rewrite the paragraph from "The History of The Strawberry Girl." Try to include as much detail as you can remember.

b. When you are finished, compare your paragraph to the original. Did you include all of the same main points? What about details — did you include as many as the original paragraph? You may want to revise your outline to include any main items you left out.

c. Try this procedure with another paragraph from any book you would like. Try to find a different type of writing, if possible. Directions, telling how to do something, are very good to outline because they make clear-cut points. Outline first, then try to rewrite the paragraph. Compare your paragraph to the original and make needed changes.

d. Optional: Choose skills from the Review Activity on the next page.

Review Activity

Write an outline of Samuel Francis Smith's life as told in "America" page 15.

✐ **Teacher's Note:** As your student completes each lesson, choose skills from the Review Activities that he needs. The Review Activities follow each lesson.

Mr. Boyer had sent word to all the neighbors that he was grinding cane. People began to drop in—the Tatums, the Cooks and others. The men went to the field where they cut the long cane stalks and hauled them in. They took turns feeding the stalks into the rollers. Cane pulp, called "pummy" fell to the ground at one side.

The pale green milky-looking cane juice poured out slowly into a barrel on the other side. Flies began to come, attracted by its sweetness. Like the flies, children and grown-ups came too, all eager to taste.

Selection reprinted from **Strawberry Girl** ©1945 by permission of the Lois Lenski Covey Foundation, Inc.

1. a. Read the literature passage silently. Ask your teacher to help you with difficult words. When you are ready, read the passage out loud to your teacher. In your own words, tell your teacher what is happening in this passage.

   b. As your teacher reads the lines in bold print out loud, write them down. Compare your copy to the literature passage and make corrections.

   c. List four to six words that you should study for spelling this week, or use the following list of suggested words: juice, barrel, poured, flies.

   > ### Spelling Tip
   > Words ending with a /l/ sound preceded by a consonant are often spelled **le** or **el**.

   Often, when words end with a /l/ sound preceded by a consonant sound, **le** is used; but sometimes the ending **el** is used. Say the words aloud as you copy them and underline **el** and **le**.

le	el
simple	barrel
angle	angel
apple	towel
trickle	tassel
pickle	nickel

2. a. Look at the simplified sentence from the literature passage:
      Children and grown-ups came, too.

      What is the complete subject?

   b. This sentence has two simple subjects. *Children* came.
      Grown-ups came. This is called a **compound subject**. The
      two simple subjects are joined by the **conjunction** *and*.

      Read the following sentences and circle the compound
      subjects.
      1) Dovey and Dan chased the Slater's hogs.
      2) Essie and Zephy were afraid of the snake.
      3) Sam and Shoestring came to play a tune.
      4) Music and laughter filled the air.
      5) Buzz and Dan went into the piney woods to gather straw.

   c. Complete the sentences with compound subjects.
      1) _____ and _____ ran across the field.
      2) _____ and _____ are my favorite colors.
      3) _____ _____ and _____ are on my pizza.
      4) _____ _____ and _____ sang a song.
      5) _____ and _____ are good friends.

   d. Write a sentence containing a compound subject.

3. a. Listen as your teacher rereads the last two sentences of
      the literature passage. The last sentence is a comparison
      of two things that shows how they are alike. This is
      called a simile (sim-elee). **Similes** use the words *like*
      or *as* to show how two things are alike. Look at the
      sentences again and tell what things are alike.

2.

a. Children and grown-ups

1) Dovey and Dan chased the Slater's hogs.
2) Essie and Zephy were afraid of the snake.
3) Sam and Shoestring came to play a tune.
4) Music and laughter filled the air.
5) Buzz and Dan went into the piney woods to gather straw.

c. Possible answers:
1) The farmer and his wife
2) Red and Blue
3) Pepperoni, mushrooms, and olives
4) Sue, Bill, and Adam
5) Melissa and Megan

d. Answers will vary.

3.
a. Children, grown-ups and flies are all attracted to sweetness.

3.

c. Children and bees are busy.
Hands and ice are cold.
"He" and the race car driver drive alike (fast).
The room and the oven feel the same (warm).

d. Answers will vary.

4.

a. Sugar cane is a common crop in Florida, Hawaii, and other places with warm climates.

b. sugar and syrup

c. Allow for discussion.

d.

1. Cut stalks from the field.
2. Haul stalks to mill.
3. Feed stalks into rollers.

e. Possible answers:
Making sugar cane takes three steps. First, you must cut stalks from the field. Next, you haul the stalks to the mill. Then you feed the stalks into the rollers.

---

b. Similes often paint word pictures to help us understand what a writer is trying to say. Read these similes to your teacher.

The children were as busy as bees.
Your hands are as cold as ice.
He drives like a race car driver.
The room feels like an oven.

c. Tell your teacher the quality that both people or things share in each simile in **3b.**

d. Make up two similes using *like* and two similes using *as*. Remember that comparing things to animals or things in nature is often a good way to start. Here are two similes with blanks in them. If you use these to help you, still make two more of each.

_____ is as gentle *as* a lamb.
_____ sleeps *like* a baby.

e. Review your spelling words.

4. **a.** Our literature passage gives us an idea of the steps involved in grinding sugar cane. Look up *sugar cane* in an encyclopedia or dictionary. What is sugar cane?

b. What do we get from sugar cane?

c. Talk with your teacher about why you think sugar cane was important to the people of Central Florida.

d. Mr. Boyer has a sugar cane mill. Make a list, using numbers, and tell the steps it takes to get *pummy* and cane juice.

e. Write a paragraph telling how to make sugar cane juice. Use your list and write complete sentences. Indent the first sentence of your paragraph. Sometimes the words *first*, *next*, and *then* (or *first*, *second*, and *thirdly*) help you write when you are telling about a step-by-step process. Look at your list after you have written your paragraph to make sure you included all the steps.

f. Optional: Take an oral or written spelling pretest.

5. a. Listen as your teacher reads the literature passage for dictation. Do not write as it is read the first time, just listen. Remember, writing from dictation is a skill you acquire with practice, like hitting a baseball. Your first attempts may not be too successful, but as you practice you will become better.

b. After you listen to the literature passage the second time, write what you have heard. When you have finished, compare your copy to the literature passage.

c. Optional: Take a spelling test.

d. Optional: Choose skills from the *Review Activities* on the next page.

✎ **Teacher's Note:** Words like *first, next,* etc. are called transitional words.

Review Activities

Choose the skills your student needs to review.

1. *Compound Subject*
   Rewrite the following sentences as one sentence with a compound subject.

   a. My sister packed a picnic lunch. I packed a picnic lunch.
   b. James fed the squirrels. John fed the squirrels.
   c. Flowers filled the hospital room. Cards filled the hospital room.
   d. The boys held a car wash. The girls held a car wash.

2. *Simile*
   Complete the sentences with a simile.

   a. Sarah was quiet as a _____.
   b. George is as brave as a _____.
   c. He acted as proud as a _____.
   d. The car was as clean as a _____.

1.
a. My sister and I packed a picnic lunch.
b. James and John fed the squirrels.
c. Flowers and cards filled the hospital room.
d. The boys and girls held a car wash.

2. Possible answers:
a. mouse
b. lion, knight
c. peacock
d. whistle

She found Dovey and took the three little girls to a shady spot under the big umbrella tree. She made play dollies out of towels for them. She brought sugar cane, peeled it down, and gave them pieces to suck and chew. She promised them candy at the candy-pulling in the evening.

With a piece of sugar cane in her mouth, she ran back to the mill. Semina was still making her obedient rounds. The mule walked with her eyes closed as if she could go on forever.

Selection reprinted from ***Strawberry Girl*** ©1945
by permission of the Lois Lenski Covey Foundation, Inc.

✎ Teacher's Note: As your student completes each lesson, choose skills from the Review Activities that he needs. The Review Activities follow each lesson.

1. a. Read the literature passage silently. Ask your teacher to help you with difficult words. When you are ready, read the passage out loud to your teacher. In your own words, tell your teacher what is happening in this passage.

   b. As your teacher reads the lines in bold print out loud, write them down. Compare your copy to the literature passage and make corrections.

   c. List four to six words that you should study for spelling this week, or use the following list of suggested words: promised, making, closed, piece.

   Today, let's review the **Spelling Tip** from Lesson 4. Before you add a suffix like **-ed** and **-ing**, look at the word. If the word ends with a silent **e,** drop the **e** and add the suffix.

> ## Spelling Tip
> Drop the silent **e** before adding a suffix beginning with a vowel.

1.

d. -ed   -ing
       hoped   hoping
       wiped   wiping
       piled   piling

2.

a. found
       took
       made
       brought
       peeled
       gave
       promised

✏ **Teacher's Note:**
To suck and chew are
verbals, and will be taught
in a higher level book.

b. present tense
      takes
      makes
      buys
      brings
      peels
      gives
      promises

c. She *finds* Davey and
     takes the three little
     girls to a shady spot
     under the big umbrella
     tree. She *makes* play
     dollies out of towels
     for them. She *brings*
     sugar cane, *peels* it
     down and *gives* them
     pieces to suck and
     chew. She *promises*
     them candy at the
     candy-pulling in the
     evening.

d. Complete the chart. Say the words aloud as you write them.

		-e	-ing
Ex:	like	liked	liking
	hope		
	wipe		
	pile		

2. a. When something has already happened, we say the verb is in the **past tense**.
       The dog runs to the house.
       (The event is happening now. - Present tense)

       The dog ran to the house.
       (The event has already happened. - Past tense)

       In our literature passage, many of the verbs are written in past tense. Find the verbs in the first paragraph, and list them vertically.

   b. Read each word on your list. These words are past tense, meaning they show that these actions have already happened. Think about each word. Next to each word on your list above, write the word that would show that the action is happening right now (present tense).
       Ex: **past tense**   **present tense**
                  found   finds

   c. Rewrite the first paragraph of our literature passage, replacing the past tense verbs from your list with the present tense verbs.

       Read it to your teacher. Make any needed corrections. Make sure each sentence sounds correct to you.

3. a. In Lesson 6, you learned about using hyphens in number
      words. Here is a list of other hyphen uses.

Use a Hyphen:
1. to connect number words from twenty-one to ninety-nine.
2. to connect fractions
3. to connect some compound words
4. to separate a word at the end of a syllable if the word
   cannot fit on a line

Look at the following words and tell why the hyphen is
used in each word.

1) jack-in-the-box
2) thirty-seven
3) one-half

b. Look at the literature passage and find the hyphenated word.
   Why is the hyphen used?

c. Look at the literature passage in Lesson 25, and find two
   words that use a hyphen. Why is the hyphen used in each?

d. Hyphens are also used to divide a word when it will not
   fit on one line, and it must be continued on the next line.
   When words are divided in this way, the hyphen must be
   used between syllables. Look at any book or newspaper.
   Find three examples of words being divided from the end
   of one line to the beginning of the next line with a hyphen.

   When you need to hyphenate a word because you do not
   have room at the end of a line, consider the following:

   1. Do not divide a one-syllable word.
   2. Divide only words of at least six letters.
      (Ex: Do not hyphenate *ta-ble*.)
   3. Do not divide a one-letter syllable from the rest of
      the word. (Ex: Do not hyphenate *abandon* like
      a-bandon; *aban-don* is better.)

3.
a. 1) jack-in-the-box
   compound word
   2) thirty-seven
   number word
   3) one-half
   fraction

b. Candy-pulling is a
   compound word.

c. milky-looking -
   compound word
   grown-ups - compound
   word

d.
1) lit-tle
2) chil-dren
3) mak-ing
4) prom-ised
5) gar-bage
6) under - don't
hyphenate

Look at the following words. Write these words, showing where each word would be hyphenated if it would not fit on one line. There is one word which should not be hyphenated.
Exa: gar/den

1) little	4) promised
2) children	5) garbage
3) making	6) under

The next time you need to hyphenate a word in your writing, remember to divide it correctly. You can check the proper place to divide the syllables of a word by looking it up in the dictionary.

e. Review your spelling words.

4. a. The main character in the story, *Strawberry Girl*, is a young girl named Birdie Boyer. Lois Lenski, the author of *Strawberry Girl*, also wrote a book of poems called *Florida, My Florida*. In this book, a poem about Birdie and her family is included. It is entitled "Cracker Girl." Listen as your teacher reads this poem. As you listen, notice how the language is different from the way you speak.

Cracker Girl
by Lois Lenski

I am a little cracker girl.
You've heard of the Florida Crackers?
Well, that's us.
Ma and Pa and five of us young uns.

Pa got us a house and a stretch o ground,
and we had us some cattle,
            a good milk cow
            a horse
            and a mule.

Right from the start we was fixin'
To make us a good livin'
a-sellin' strawberries,
            oranges,
            sweet 'taters
            and sugar cane.
We plowed our field and fenced it,
We planted berries there.
We fought to keep the hogs out
            as hard as we could dare.

Our neighbors made a ruckus.
Them Slaters made a fuss.
But Ma --
            she was the one to show 'em.
Our way, it was the best.

Selection reprinted from *Florida, My Florida* by
permission of the Lois Lenski Covey Foundation, Inc.

b. Read the poem silently after your teacher has read it.
Ask your teacher about any words or expressions that
are unknown to you. Then read the poem aloud to your
teacher. Practice a few times. How does it feel to read
language that is different? What words or phrases sound
different? This type of language is called informal, slang,
or **dialect**. That means it is language that is written in the
same way a people from a certain part of the country, a
certain time period, or a certain culture might speak. It is
different from standard English we use in most speaking
and writing. It often shows us a unique quality of a
group of people.

Talk with your teacher about the area where you live. Are there any examples of unique dialects around you? See if you can find stories or poems written in a dialect or informal language common to your area. Your librarian may be able to help you find such poems or stories.

c. Practice reading "Cracker Girl," and present it to your family. Try to read it with expression in your voice as if you were speaking in your own dialect.

d. Optional: Take an oral or written spelling pretest.

5. a. Listen as your teacher reads the literature passage for dictation. Do not write as it is read the first time, just listen. Remember, writing from dictation is a skill you acquire with practice, like hitting a baseball. Your first attempts may not be too successful, but as you practice you will become better.

b. After you listen to the literature passage the second time, write what you have heard. When you have finished, compare your copy to the literature passage.

c. Take a spelling test.

d. Optional: Choose skills from the *Review Activities* on the next page.

Review Activities

Choose the skills your student needs to review.

1. *Verb Tense*
   The verbs listed are in the past tense. Write them in the present tense.

   a. carried
   b. melted
   c. hoped
   d. tried
   e. fought
   f. swam

2. *Syllables*
   Divide each word into syllables.

   a. simple
   b. marble
   c. relish
   d. fountain
   e. cactus
   f. storage

1.
a. **carry (carries)**
b. **melt (s)**
c. **hope (s)**
d. **try (tries)**
e. **fight (s)**
f. **swim (s)**

2.
a. **sim - ple**
b. **mar - ble**
c. **rel- ish**
d. **foun - tain**
e. **cac- tus**
f. **stor - age**

Teacher's Note: As your student completes each lesson, choose skills from the Review Activities that he needs. The Review Activities follow each lesson.

Sam Slater and Gus and Joe appeared. No frolic was complete without them. Sam brought his fiddle into the house and struck up a lively tune, while Shoestring stood at his side and picked on the violin strings with knitting needles, for an accompaniment. **The men and women formed into lines, and Sam Slater called the dance steps in a loud voice. Soon the rooms and porches were a flurry of movement, music, and laughter.** *Joe Slater danced fancy steps, and made the people laugh. "He shore can cut the fool!" they said.*

Selection reprinted from ***Strawberry Girl*** ©1945 by permission of the Lois Lenski Covey Foundation, Inc.

1. a. Read the literature passage silently. Ask your teacher to help you with difficult words. When you are ready, read the passage out loud to your teacher. In your own words, tell your teacher what is happening in this passage.

   b. As your teacher reads the lines in bold print out loud, write them down. Compare your copy to the literature passage and make corrections.

   c. List four to six words that you should study for spelling this week, or use the following list of suggested words: flurry, movement, laughter, dance.

   Some words like *laughter* are spelled with **gh** to make a **/f/** sound. Look at the following words. Copy the words and underline **gh**. Say the words aloud as you write them.

> ### Spelling Tip
> Some words like laugh are spelled with **gh** to make a **/f/** sound.

laughter	cough	rough
drought	enough	tough

2. a. Look at the simplified sentence from the literature passage: Sam brought his fiddle into the house and struck up a lively tune.

   Draw a vertical line between the complete subject and predicate. Underline the subject once and underline the verb twice.

   Perhaps you had a hard time finding the verb because there are two verbs in this sentence. The subject *Sam* did two things: Sam *brought* and *struck*. The two verbs are joined by the **conjunction** *and*. When a simple sentence has two or more verbs, it is called a **compound verb**.

   b. Let's review a compound subject.
      Ex: The men and women formed lines.
            The sentence has two subjects, *men* and *women*.

   c. Now, let's review a compound sentence.
      Ex: They formed lines, and Sam Slater called dance steps. *They formed lines* is a complete sentence. *They* is subject; *formed* is the verb. *Sam Slater called dance steps* is also a complete sentence. *Sam Slater* is the subject; *called* is the verb. The two sentences are joined by a comma and the conjunction, *and*.

   d. Read the sentences, and write **CV** (compound verb), **CSub** (compound subject), or **CSent** (compound sentence).

      1) Birdie swept the front porch and washed the clothes.
      2) Dan and Davey watered the garden.
      3) The fire was lit, and the syrup making began.
      4) A crowd of people danced and talked.
      5) We raise strawberries and sell them.

   e. People who lived in the pioneer days of any land realized they had to depend on each other for help in times of need and for fun and fellowship. The Slater family causes considerable trouble for the families in the area, particularly the Boyers. This festive event (called a frolic) is being held at the Boyer home, and the Slater boys— Sam, Gus, and Joe are there. Read the literature passage again. How did the Slaters participate in the frolic?

2.

a. Sam / <u>brought</u> his fiddle into the house and <u>struck</u> up a lively tune.

d. 1) CV
   2) CSub.
   3) CSent.
   4) CV
   5) CV

e. The Slaters were a main part of the event, playing music, calling the dance steps and leading the dance.

f. The dancing they are doing is probably similar to what we know as square dancing. Look this up in an encyclopedia and tell your teacher some of the main elements of square dancing—such as how it is done, what kind of music is used, etc.

g. If you have an opportunity, observe or participate in a square dance with your parents' permission and/or by accompanying them. If possible, view a video that shows basic square dancing.

h. How do you think this type of event was helpful to pioneer people?

3. a. Listen as your teacher reads the poem entitled "Beholden" by Lois Lenski. Read the poem silently after your teacher has read it. Looking at the poem, make a list of all the words that seem unusual in their spelling or pronunciation.

h. Possible answer: The pioneer life was a hard life full of work, and the people seldom had a chance to get together for relaxation and recreation. These opportunities became important times for pioneer families.

3.
a. Hit, beholden, porely, young uns, full o meanness, bygones

Beholden
by Lois Lenski

Hit pulled my heart out nearly
    To have to send for you;
Don't like to be beholden
    For all the good you do.

But when I'm sick and porely,
    The young uns cryin' too—
If I can't call my neighbor,
    Good Lord! What would I do?

I know we're full o meanness,
    And you been kind and good;
So let's forget our bygones
    Just like a body should.

Selection reprinted from *Florida, My Florida* by permission of the Lois Lenski Covey Foundation, Inc.

b. Talk with your teacher and come up with definitions for each of these dialectal words.

c. Rewrite the poem putting your own words in place of the words on your list. Do you think the poem sounds better with your words, or with the original words?

d. Count the number of syllables in each line of the poem "Beholden" and write down the numbers. What is the pattern for each group of four lines?

e. Think of a familiar topic and try to write four lines about it, following the same syllable pattern, or find another poem that follows the same pattern.

f. Review your spelling words.

4. a. Reread the poem "Cracker Girl" by Lois Lenski on page 203. Look at the last four lines of this poem. The neighbors referred to by Birdie in this poem are the Slaters. What does Birdie say about her mother?

b. In the poem, "Beholden," the poem refers to "my neighbor." Who do you think are the neighbors?

c. Jesus said "Do unto others as you would have them do unto you." (Luke 6:31) People today call this the "Golden Rule." Mrs. Boyer has been demonstrating the Golden Rule in her relationship with the Slaters by doing kind things for them. What do you think has been the effect of her kindness? Discuss the Golden Rule with your teacher.

d. Write the Golden Rule on a sheet of paper or on your *Student Activity Book* on page 243.

e. Can you think of a situation in your life to which you can apply the Golden Rule?

f. Do you think it is always easy to do this? Talk with your teacher about ways you can apply the Golden Rule to a specific situation. You may want to write about that situation, then write about the situation later and tell the results of applying the Golden Rule.

---

b. **Hit-it**
   beholden-obliged
   porely-feeling badly
   young uns-young ones
   full o meaness-full of meaness
   bygones-quarrels from the past

c. **Answers will vary.**

d. **7, 6, 7, 6**

e. **Answers will vary.**

4.
a. **Her mother showed them a better way.**

b. **The Slaters and the Boyers.**

c. **Answers will vary.**

d. **self-explanatory**

e. **Allow for discussion**

f. **Answers will vary.**

g. Optional: Take an oral or written spelling pretest.

5. a. Listen as your teacher reads the literature passage for dictation. Do not write as it is read the first time, just listen. Remember, writing from dictation is a skill you acquire with practice, like hitting a baseball. Your first attempts may not be too successful, but as you practice you will become better.

   b. After you listen to the literature passage the second time, write what you have heard. When you have finished, compare your copy to the literature passage.

   c. Optional: Take a spelling test.

   d. Optional: Choose skills from the *Review Activities* on the next page.

Review Activities

Choose the skills your student needs to review.

1. *Compound Verb, Compound Subject, Compound Sentence*
   Read the sentences, and write **CV** (compound verb), **CSub** (compound subject), or **CSent** (compound sentence).

   a. Ellen sat in her chair and looked out the window.
   b. Mom and Dad came home early.
   c. We swam and played at the beach.
   d. Jason came early, but Carl was late.
   e. Every morning we pray together and read the Bible.
   f. Cindy went with Cathy, and I went with Dana.
   g. My brother and sister set up a lemonade stand.

2. *Poetry*

   Read aloud the poem "Cracker Girl" on page 203 or "Beholden," on page 208.

1.
a. **CV**
b. **CSub**
c. **CV**
d. **CSent**
e. **CV**
f. **CSent**
g. **CSub**

Teacher's Note: As your student completes each lesson, choose skills from the Review Activities that he needs. The Review Activities follow each lesson.

Meanwhile Mr. Boyer had set fire to a pine stump nearby. **When darkness came down, he had a great bonfire burning to light up the yard.** *The boys ran to pile on more lightwood knots whenever it burned low.* **It hissed and crackled and popped, bathing the dancing figures in a pattern of light and shadow.**

Mr. Boyer made the candy himself. He boiled the syrup down to just the right temperature, then poured the thickening mixture out on many plates to cool.

Birdie took plates to the little Slater girls and Dovey and showed them how to pull.

Selection reprinted from ***Strawberry Girl*** ©1945 by permission of the Lois Lenski Covey Foundation, Inc.

1. a. Read the literature passage silently. Ask your teacher to help you with difficult words. When you are ready, read the passage out loud to your teacher. In your own words, tell your teacher what is happening in this passage.

   b. As your teacher reads the lines in bold print out loud, write them down. Compare your copy to the literature passage and make corrections.

   c. List four to six words that you should study for spelling this week, or use the following list of suggested words: crackled, figures, shadow, pattern.

   Often, words ending with the long /o/ sound are spelled with **ow**.

   > ### Spelling Tip
   > Often words ending with a long */o/* sound are spelled with **ow**, as in shadow.

   Say the words aloud as you write them. Underline the **ow**.

shadow	window	glow
below	mow	meadow

2. a. Compound words are made up of two separate words put together to form a new word such as *baseball*. There are five compound words in our literature passage. Point them out to your teacher.

   b. Two of our compound words have meanings that are very interesting. Look up the words *bonfire* and *lightwood* in the dictionary. After reading the definitions, tell your teacher what these words mean.

   c. Bonfires can be fun, and the boys seem very excited as they run to add wood to the fire. Sometimes, things can be described by using descriptive verbs. Read the fourth sentence in the literature passage. What three descriptive verbs describe the bonfire?

   d. Read the following sentences and replace the verb with a descriptive verb. You may choose a word from the *Descriptive Verb Box* or think of your own.

Descriptive Verb Box		
grinned	smirked	collapsed
lounged	trickled	trudged
plodded	pounded	rested
beat	whined	whimpered

1) He *walked* through the snowstorm.
2) The rain *fell* on the roof.
3) The curious boy *smiled*.
4) She *sat* on the couch.
5) The baby *cried*.

2.
a. meanwhile, bonfire, lightwood, whenever, himself.

b. bonfire - a large outdoor fire
   lightwood - resinous wood that burns brightly

c. hissed, crackled, and popped.

d. Possible answers:
   1) trudged
   2) pounded
   3) grinned
   4) rested
   5) whimpered

3. a. In times past, agricultural communities often got together for events relating to harvest time. This literature passage describes a farming community getting together to participate, and celebrate harvesting the sugar cane crop. As part of the fun, candy was made with the boiled cane juice.

Everyone took a plate of the cooling mixture, which had to be "pulled" to get it ready to eat. Ask if you can make one of these types of candy, with your teacher's assistance and supervision. One recipe that would be very similar to the candy-pulling in our literature passage would be saltwater taffy. Many cookbooks have recipes for taffy.

Salt Water Taffy

1 cup sugar
$3/4$ cup light corn syrup
$2/3$ cup water
1 tablespoon cornstarch
2 tablespoons butter or margarine
1 teaspoon salt
2 teaspoons vanilla

Butter square pan, 8x8x2 inches. In 2-quart saucepan, combine sugar, corn syrup, water, cornstarch, butter and salt. Cook over medium heat, stirring constantly, to 256° on candy thermometer (or until small amount of mixture dropped into very cold water forms a hard ball). Remove from heat; stir in vanilla. Pour into pan.

When just cool enough to handle, pull taffy until satiny, light in color and stiff. If taffy becomes sticky, butter hands lightly. Pull into long strips, $1/2$ inch wide. With scissors, cut strips into 1-inch pieces. Wrap pieces individually in plastic wrap or waxed paper. (Candy must be wrapped to hold shape.) Makes about 1 pound.

---

b. Review your spelling words.

4. a. Yesterday you used a recipe to make candy. Recipes are written so that you understand what to do step-by-step. Reread recipe you used to make the candy.

 b. Without copying the recipe, use your own words to write several sentences that tell someone how to make the candy you made yesterday. Use transitive words like *first*, *secondly*, *next*, *finally*, etc. Be as specific as you need to, so that someone else would know exactly what to do.

 c. Give your directions and the recipe to your teacher, and ask if you have included all the necessary steps. The best test of your directions would be for someone to use them as directions and try to make the same candy you made. The final test of your directions will be how the candy tastes.

 d. Optional: Take an oral or written spelling pretest.

5. a. Listen as your teacher reads the literature passage for dictation. Do not write as it is read the first time, just listen. Remember, writing from dictation is a skill you acquire with practice, like hitting a baseball. Your first attempts may not be too successful, but as you practice you will become better.

 b. After you listen to the literature passage the second time, write what you have heard. When you have finished, compare your copy to the literature passage.

 c. Optional: Take a spelling test.

 d. Optional: Choose skills from the *Review Activities* on the next page.

Review Activities

Choose the skills your student needs to review.

1. *Descriptive Verbs*
   Replace the italicized verb with a more descriptive verb.

   a. My neighbor *smiled*.
   b. The stranger *walked* away.
   c. The boy *cried*.
   d. The diamond *shone*.
   e. The young man closed his eyes and *thought*.

2. *Directions*
   Write step-by-step directions for any of the following:

   a. How to bathe a dog.
   b. How to make a sandwich.
   c. How to make your bed.
   d. How to wash the dishes.

---

1. **Possible answers:**
   a. grinned, smirked
   b. drifted, strolled
   c. bawled, whimpered, wept, wailed, sobbed
   d. glimmered, glistened, sparkled
   e. reflected, pondered

2. **Answers will vary.**

Assessment 5
(Lessons 24 - 28)

1. Rewrite the following sentences as one sentence by using a conjunction and a compound subject

   a. Dad went on vacation. Mom went on vacation.
   b. The dog slept on the porch. The cat slept on the porch.
   c. Robert woke up. Ted woke up.

2. Give an example of a simile.

3. The verbs listed are in the present tense. Write them in the past tense.

   a. fight
   b. hope
   c. melt

4. Divide each word into syllables.

   a. table
   b. garden
   c. sample

5. Add hyphens to these number words as needed. (Some words do not need hyphens.)

   a. ninety eight
   b. one hundred
   c. thirty six
   d. five hundred sixty eight

1.
a. **Dad and Mom went on vacation.**
b. **The dog and cat slept on the porch.**
c. **Robert and Ted woke up.**

2. Possible answers: smooth as silk, soft as a feather, etc.

3.
a. **fought**
b. **hoped**
c. **melted**

4.
a. **ta ble**
b. **gar den**
c. **sam ple**

5.
a. **ninety-eight**
b. **no hyphen needed**
c. **thirty-six**
d. **five hundred sixty-eight**

EVERYDAY WORDS

in
Amos Fortune, Free Man

Teacher's Note: As your student completes each lesson, choose skills from the Review Activities that he needs. The Review Activities follow each lesson.

Amos and Violet slept under the stars while peepers chimed in a marsh nearby, and late birds called to each other. They were free. **They were starting life anew. They were being helped to get going, and the people in the land to which they had come were showing gladness at their arrival.**

"God give me strength for many years to do my work well," *Amos prayed in the quiet of his heart.*

From ***Amos Fortune, Free Man*** by Elizabeth Yates, cover by Lonnie Knabel.
©1950 by Elizabeth Yates McGreal, Renewed ©1978 by Elizabeth Yates McGreal.
Used by permission of Dutton Children's Books, a division of Pengnin Books USA, Inc.

1. a. Read the literature passage silently. Ask your teacher to help you with difficult words. When you are ready, read the passage out loud to your teacher. In your own words, tell your teacher what is happening in this passage.

   b. As your teacher reads the lines in bold print out loud, write them down. Compare your copy to the literature passage and make corrections.

   c. List four to six words that you should study for spelling this week, or use the following list of suggested words: they, which, were, their.

2.

a. Amos and Violet

b. Compound subject

2. a. Look at the first sentence of the literature passage. What is the subject?

   b. Do you remember what this kind of subject is called?

   If Amos was speaking, he would say, "*Violet and I* slept under the stars." A common mistake is made in using the incorrect pronoun.

   Violet and me slept under the stars. This incorrect.

One way to decide which pronoun to use is by referring to your Personal Pronoun Chart on page 14. If the pronoun is the subject, use a pronoun in the subjective case. An easier way to tell which pronoun to use is by simply taking out the other subject.

Read the sentence without *Violet*.
> *Me* slept under the stars.
> *I* slept under the stars.

Which sounds correct? *I* sounds correct, so say *Violet and I* slept under the stars.

c. Use the same method when deciding which pronoun to use in the objective case.
Ex: Freedom gave Violet and (*I or me*) a new life.

Read the sentence without *Violet*.
> Freedom gave *I* a new life. (It doesn't sound correct)
> Freedom gave *me* a new life. (It sounds correct)

Therefore the following is correct.
> Freedom gave me a new life. (It sounds correct)

d. Choose the correct pronoun.

1) Mother laughed at Jack and (I, me).
2) As Brian and (I, me) left, it started raining.
3) The dog chased Sarah and (I, me).
4) Casey and (I, me) are running in a race.
5) Our new sneakers gave Tom and (I, me) blisters.
6) On Wednesday, my dad and (I, me) are going fishing.
7) Karen came with Joshua and (I, me) to the beach.
8) Jason, Cory, and (I, me) are on the swim team.

2.
d. 1) me
   2) I
   3) me
   4) I
   5) me
   6) I
   7) me
   8) I

3. a. This story is a **biography** (a true story about someone's life). Read the biographical information in the following paragraph and make a time line showing Amos Fortune's life. (Use the same procedure we used in Lesson 5, **2c**.)

3.
b.

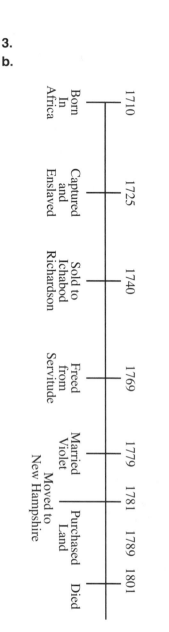

4.
a. Answers will vary.

b. Answers will vary.

Amos Fortune was born in 1710 in Africa. He was captured and enslaved in 1725 at the age of 15. He was purchased at that time by the Copeland family of Boston, Massachusetts, who were Quaker. In 1740, Mr. Copeland died and Amos was sold to Mr. Ichabod Richardson of Woburn, Massachusetts. Amos was freed from servitude in 1769. He and Violet were married in 1779, on the day after he purchased her freedom. In 1781 he and Violet moved to Jaffrey, New Hampshire. In 1789, Amos purchased 25 acres of land, becoming a landowner. Amos Fortune died in 1801, at the age 91.

b. Add to your time line any other important dates such as the dates of the Revolutionary War and Independence Day.

c. Review your spelling words.

4. a. Amos and Violet were slaves for many years. Though the families that Amos lived with, the Copelands and the Richardsons, were kind to him, he was still unable to go where he pleased, or do as he pleased. In previous lessons, you have looked up the definitions of such words as *liberty* and *freedom*. Now look up the words *slave* and *slavery*. Tell your teacher what these words mean. How do you think it would feel to be a slave? Talk with your teacher about your answer.

b. Even though Amos was enslaved, he served his masters with obedience, loyalty, and service beyond what the law required of him. Why do you think Amos served his masters and their families so well?

c. Optional: Take an oral or written spelling pretest.

5. a. Listen as your teacher reads the literature passage for
       dictation. Do not write as it is read the first time, just
       listen. Remember, writing from dictation is a skill you
       acquire with practice, like hitting a baseball. Your first
       attempts may not be too successful, but as you practice
       you will become better.

   b. After you listen to the literature passage the second time,
       write what you have heard. When you have finished,
       compare your copy to the literature passage.

   c. Optional: Take a spelling test.

   d. Optional: Choose skills from the *Review Activities* on the
       next page.

Review Activities

Choose the skills your student needs to review.

1. a. I
  b. me
  c. I
  d. I
  e. me

1. *Pronouns*
   Complete the sentences with the correct pronoun.

   a. Martha and (I, me) baked two dozen cookies.
   b. The boys asked Martha and (I, me) if they could have some.
   c. Ramon, Peter, and (I, me) waited for the bus.
   d. My brother and (I, me) went fishing.
   e. Uncle Robert asked Brian and (I, me) to go with him.

2. A biography is a true story about someone's life.

2. *Biography*
   What is a biography?

Ever since he had his freedom he had saved one small fortune and then another. Now he wanted to spend once more the hard-earned savings in the iron kettle, and Violet would not let him. **What right had she to oppose him? Yet it was he who had given her freedom. The word was meaningless unless in its light each one lived up to his highest and his best.**

"Oh, Lord," Amos said, "You've always got an answer and You're always ready to give it to the man who trusts You. Keep me open-hearted this night so when it comes I'll know it's You speaking and I'll heed what You have to say."

From ***Amos Fortune, Free Man*** by Elizabeth Yates, cover by Lonnie Knabel. ©1950 by Elizabeth Yates McGreal, Renewed ©1978 by Elizabeth Yates McGreal. Used by permission of Dutton Children's Books, a division of Pengnin Books USA, Inc.

 Teacher's Note: As your student completes each lesson, choose skills from the Review Activities that he needs. The Review Activities follow each lesson.

1. a. Read the literature passage silently. Ask your teacher to help you with difficult words. When you are ready, read the passage out loud to your teacher. In your own words, tell your teacher what is happening in this passage.

   b. As your teacher reads the lines in bold print out loud, write them down. Compare your copy to the literature passage and make corrections.

   c. List four to six words that you should study for spelling this week, or use the following list of suggested words: oppose, freedom, meaningless, highest.

   Today, let's review the **Spelling Tip** from Lesson 2.

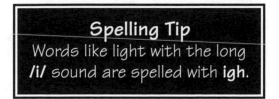

Spelling Tip
Words like light with the long /i/ sound are spelled with **igh**.

   d. Find three words in the literature passage which follow this **Spelling Tip**, and write them down.

1.
d. right, light, high

2.

a. They begin with a capital letter.

b. You've, You're, You, You, You

c. 1) I am encouraged to read God's Word daily.
2) Jesus spoke to His disciples.
3) Jesus is the Son of God.
4) Jesus, the Prince of Peace, gives me hope for everyday.

e. unimportant or without meaning

f. hopeless - without hope
homeless - without a home
weightless - without weight
sleepless - without sleep

g. Answers will vary.

h. Answers will vary.

---

2. a. Look at the last paragraph of the literature passage. What do you notice about the words *you* and *you're* in the passage?

b. Words referring to God and the Bible are always capitalized. Circle all the words and pronouns referring to God.

c. Capitalize words referring to God and the Bible.

   1) I am encouraged to read god's word daily.
   2) jesus spoke to his disciples.
   3) jesus is the son of god.
   4) jesus, the prince of peace, gives me hope for everyday.

d. Remember our picture of base words with prefixes and suffixes? Here it is again.

The main house is the base word. The garage on the left is a prefix (letters added to the beginning of a word). The extra room on the right is a suffix (letters added to the end of a word). Both prefixes and suffixes change the meaning of the base word.

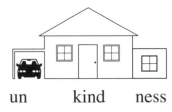

un   kind   ness

e. The last sentence of the first paragraph in the literature passage begins, "The word was meaningless..." The suffix **-less** means without. What do you think the word *meaningless* means?

f. Add the suffix **-less** to the following words and then tell what you think they mean. Look up any words you do not know.

   hope   home   weight   sleep

g. Make up a sentence, orally or in writing, using each new word.

h. See if you can think of more words that have the suffix **-less**.

3. a. What you see in the literature passage can be described as a conflict, or problem. Most stories have at least one conflict (or problem), which is solved in the story. In your own words, tell your teacher what you think is the conflict between Amos and Violet.

   b. Actually, there is more to this conflict. Amos wants to spend the money to help another poor family, and Violet wants him to use it to purchase his lifelong dream of owning his own home and land. She is not trying to be selfish. She thinks Amos has been very unselfish, and wants him to see the result of all his hard work. Without looking or reading ahead, tell what you think is going to happen next.

   c. There are ways that you can predict, or tell beforehand, what might happen in a story. This is called **predicting outcome**. What we know about a character—how they have acted before, help us predict outcome. Circumstances and events in a story also give us ideas as to what will happen next. When you are reading, stop during a story and decide what you think will happen next. Then read on and see if you were right. Compare your ending to what really happened.

   d. Here are some simple circumstances. Try to predict what you think will happen next, based on what you already know.

      1) It rains for days and days. The river is rising. The weather forecast calls for more rain. What could happen next? Think of more than one possibility.

      2) The policeman saw a man outside a closed store. The man was looking around. The man walked over to the door knob and tried to open the door. What do you think will happen next? Think of more than one possible answer.

      3) A woman and three little children are at a park. The children are playing and the woman is smiling and watching them. One of the children falls down and starts to cry. What will happen next? Think of several possible answers.

3.
a. Amos wants to spend the money and Violet does not.

b. Answers will vary.

d. 1) The river floods its bank; the river rises to the top of the bank and the rain stops; workers come and open floodgates so the river goes down.
2) The man tries to rob the store and gets caught; the man left his wallet inside and is worried about getting it back; the man's car won't start and he is trying to get help.
3) The woman picks up and comforts her child; one of the other children helps the child; the child gets up and goes to the woman for comfort.

3.
e. Answers will vary.

4.
a. He prays for God's direction to be made real to him.

b. Yes

c. Amos left the final decision up to God.

d. Answers will vary.

e. Answers will vary.

e. Choose one of the situations in **3d** and write a conclusion to it.

f. Review your spelling words.

4. a. When Amos has not known what to do, or when he needed help in the past, he has often done the same thing. What does he do in this week's literature passage when faced with uncertainty about what to do?

b. Has Amos prayed before? (Look at the literature passage in Lesson 28).

c. By praying, Amos is saying that the final decision about what he does in his life is not up to him. Who has he left it up to?

d. Talk with your teacher about times in her life when important decisions had to be made. How did she go about making them? Have you ever had to make decisions that were important to you? How did you make those decisions?

e. Think of a three or four step plan for making decisions. Write down your plan and put it where you can look at it if you need it. You may want to write it like this, using simple directions.

Step 1.   Talk to Mom and Dad.
Step 2.   Pray about it.
Step 3.   See if the Bible says anything about it.
Step 4.   Talk with Mom and Dad again, asking if my decision is alright with them.

f. The Bible gives us a prayer that Jesus taught the disciples which asks for God's will or plan, to be done each day. Listen as your teacher reads Matthew 6:7-15. Included in this Scripture is a section called The Lord's Prayer. It contains verses 9-13. Talk with your teacher about what this prayer means. If you have not yet memorized the Lord's Prayer, this would be a good time to learn it.

The Lord's Prayer

Our Father who art in heaven,
Hallowed be Thy name.
Thy Kingdom come.
Thy will be done,
On earth, as it is in heaven.
Give us this day our daily bread.
And forgive us our debts, as we also have forgiven
    our debtors.
And do not lead us into temptation,
But deliver us from evil.

Note: Your family may use another translation of the Bible, or say this prayer in a slightly different way.

g. Optional: Take an oral or written spelling pretest.

5. a. Listen as your teacher reads the literature passage for dictation. Do not write as it is read the first time, just listen. Remember, writing from dictation is a skill you acquire with practice, like hitting a baseball. Your first attempts may not be too successful, but as you practice you will become better.

   b. After you listen to the literature passage the second time, write what you have heard. When you have finished, compare your copy to the literature passage.

   c. Optional: Take a spelling test.

   d. Optional: Choose skills from the *Review Activities* on the next page.

Review Activities

Choose the skills your student needs to review.

1. *Capitalization (Words referring to God)*
   Add capitalization.

   a. the lord is compassionate and gracious.
   b. the lord is my savior.
   c. we praise our lord almighty.
   d. god alone is the holy one.
   e. the word became flesh and lived among us.
   f. the scripture cannot be broken.

2. *Suffix -less*
   Add the suffix **-less** to the following words.

   a. help
   h. care
   c. shame
   d. cord
   e. hair
   f. point

3. What does the suffix **-less** mean?

1.
a. **The Lord is compassionate and gracious.**
b. **The Lord is my Savior.**
c. **We praise our Lord Almighty.**
d. **God alone is the Holy One.**
e. **The Word became flesh and lived among us.**
f. **The Scripture cannot be broken.**

2.
a. **helpless**
b. **careless**
c. **shameless**
d. **cordless**
e. **hairless**
f. **pointless**

3. without

That afternoon Amos and Violet rode over to William Turner's and signed the deed that put twenty-five acres of land, cleared and forest with a brook running through it, in Amos Fortune's name.

And there, by the bank of the brook, Amos built his own house—strong enough to meet the stress of time and the force of storms. He built a barn and a tanyard and excavated basins in the brook for his work.

By the end of 1789, when Amos Fortune was in his eightieth year, he became a land owner in his own right, and one of his life's long dreams was fulfilled.

From ***Amos Fortune, Free Man*** by Elizabeth Yates, cover by Lonnie Knabel.
©1950 by Elizabeth Yates McGreal, Renewed ©1978 by Elizabeth Yates McGreal.
Used by permission of Dutton Children's Books, a division of Pengnin Books USA, Inc.

Teacher's Note: As your student completes each lesson, choose skills from the Review Activities that he needs. The Review Activities follow each lesson.

1. a. Read the literature passage silently. Ask your teacher to help you with difficult words. When you are ready, read the passage out loud to your teacher. In your own words, tell your teacher what is happening in this passage.

   b. As your teacher reads the lines in bold print out loud, write them down. Compare your copy to the literature passage and make corrections.

   c. List four to six words that you should study for spelling this week, or use the following list of suggested words: eightieth, owner, right, fulfilled.

   d. In Lesson 20, you learned to change the **y** to **i** before adding the suffix **-ness**. The same rule applies when adding any other suffix, except **-ing** to words ending in **y** preceded by a consonant.

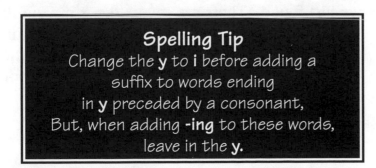

Spelling Tip
Change the **y** to **i** before adding a suffix to words ending in **y** preceded by a consonant, But, when adding **-ing** to these words, leave in the **y**.

e. Copy the following words. Say the words aloud as you write them.

eighty	eightieth
plenty	plentiful
heavy	heaviest
pretty	prettier
hurry	hurrying
rally	rallying

2. a. Look at the third paragraph of the literature passage. When writing dates in a sentence, remember to use correct punctuation.

   Ex: My sister was born on September 16, 1981, in North Carolina.

b. Add correct punctuation.

   1) Ron moved in with his grandparents on August 10 1995.
   2) On October 15 1996 I planted a garden.
   3) The deadline for the poetry contest was February 20 1994.

c. A dictionary can give you much information about a word. Here is a sample of a dictionary entry. Read it silently as your teacher reads aloud, or you may read it aloud.

   ①   ②   ③ ④   ⑤   ⑥
   own • er (ō ′ n ə r), *n.* the one who owns: *Who is the owner of this car?*

   Look at the entry and tell what information is given for each number in the entry.

d. Look in your dictionary and find an entry for any other word. Locate the same six pieces of information that we just found. There are several keys in your dictionary that can help you. With your teacher's help, find the pronunciation key and the key to the abbreviations for the parts of speech. Talk with your teacher about your dictionary.

2.
1) Ron moved in with his grandparents on August 10,1995.
2) On October 15, 1996, I planted a garden.
3) The deadline for the poetry contest was February 20, 1994.

✏ Teacher's Note: Dictionary entries may vary.

c.
1) how to spell it
2) how many syllables it has and where to divide them
3) how to pronounce the word
4) what part of speech it is
5) what it means
6) how to use it in a sentence

e. Another very important piece of information about using a dictionary tells you how to find the word you want. There are words at the top of each page called **guide words**. All of the words in the dictionary are in alphabetical order. Look at the guide words to find the page containing your word. Look throughout the dictionary reading some guide words. Answer these questions after looking through your dictionary.

1) What word is listed on the top left-hand corner of each page?
2) What word is listed on the upper right-hand corner of the page?
3) Would the word *camper* be on the page with these guide words—*calm* and *campground*?
4) Would *play* be on the page with these guide words—*plastic* and *plausible*?
5) Find the word *literature* in your dictionary. What are the guide words on that page?

f. Dictionaries give us more information about words than just what they mean. Use your dictionary and look up these words.

deed	bank	toward
stress	excavate	basin

Answer the following questions orally about each word:

1) What are the guide words for the page this word is on?
2) How many syllables are in this word?
3) How many meanings does this word have?
4) What does this word mean?

3. a. In Lesson 5 you learned how to write a friendly letter. Write a letter to a friend or relative. You may refer back to Lesson 15 for help with your friendly letter and addressing an envelope.

b. Review your spelling words.

4. a. This literature passage paints a very clear picture of the land

---

2.
e. 1) The first word listed on the page.
   2) The last word listed on the page.
   3) Yes
   4) No
   5) Answers will vary.

✏ Teacher's Note: Dictionaries may vary, so teach your student accordingly.

f. Consult your dictionary

4.

a. 64 years

b. 1) If you love money, you won't be satisfied with it, even if you get more.
2) God asks if we will rob Him of the tithes and offerings we owe Him. He will bless our giving.
3) However you give to others is the way blessings will be given to you.
4) A person who works is worthy to receive his wages.
5) It is more blessed to give than to receive.
6) The love of money is the root (beginning of) all kinds of evils.

Allow time for discussion.

c. Answers will vary.

that Amos Fortune bought from William Turner. Look back at the time line you made in Lesson 29, **3b**. How many years did Amos work after coming to America before he was able to purchase his own home?

Amos could have purchased land sooner, had he not used his money to help others so often.

b. What does the Bible have to say about money? How do you know when you are to save your money, and when you should spend it? These are important questions we all have to think about. After reading each Scripture with your teacher, tell in your own words what you think the main point is of each Scripture.

1) Ecclesiastes 5:10
2) Malachi 3:8-10
3) Luke 6:38
4) Luke 10:7
5) Acts 20:35
6) I Timothy 6:9-10

c. After discussion, write a paragraph or two that tells what you believe about money and what you will do with it.

d. Optional: Take an oral or written spelling pretest.

5. a. Listen as your teacher reads the literature passage for dictation. Do not write as it is read the first time, just listen. Remember, writing from dictation is a skill you acquire with practice, like hitting a baseball. Your first attempts may not be too successful, but as you practice you will become better.

b. After you listen to the literature passage the second time, write what you have heard. When you have finished, compare your copy to the literature passage.

c. Optional: Take a spelling test.

d. Optional: Choose skills from the *Review Activities* on the next page.

Review Activities

Choose the skills your student needs to review.

1. *Dates - Punctuation*
   Add punctuation as needed.

   a. My library book is due on May 14 1996.
   b. On June 22 1994 my baby brother was born.
   e. On November 30 1990 we moved into our new house.

2. *Dictionary*

   a. What information does a dictionary give you?
   b. What are guide words, and how do they help you find a word in a dictionary?

1.

a. My library book is due on May 14, 1996.

b. On June 22,1994, my baby brother was born.

c. On November 30, 1990, we moved into our new house.

2.

a. A dictionary gives you the correct spelling, definition, pronunciation, syllabication and also tells you the part of speech. Sometimes it gives a picture and is used in a sentence.

b. Guide words are the first and last words listed on a dictionary page. This helps you know if the word you are looking up is on that page.

✏️ **Teacher's Note:** As your student completes each lesson, choose skills from the Review Activities that he needs. The Review Activities follow each lesson.

"Once, long years ago, I thought I could set a canoe-load of my people free by breaking the bands at my wrists and killing the white man who held the weapon. I had the strength in my hands to do such a deed and I had the fire within, but I didn't do it."

"What held you back?"

Amos shook his head. "My hand was restrained and I'm glad that it was, for the years between have shown me that it does a man no good to be free until he knows how to live, how to walk in step with God."

From *Amos Fortune, Free Man* by Elizabeth Yates, cover by Lonnie Knabel.
©1950 by Elizabeth Yates McGreal, Renewed ©1978 by Elizabeth Yates McGreal.
Used by permission of Dutton Children's Books, a division of Pengnin Books USA, Inc.

1. a. Read the literature passage silently. Ask your teacher to help you with difficult words. When you are ready, read the passage out loud to your teacher. Narrate to your teacher what is happening in this passage.

   b. As your teacher reads the lines in bold print out loud, write them down. Compare your copy to the literature passage and make corrections.

   c. List four to six words that you should study for spelling this week, or use the following list of suggested words: restrained, between, shown, until. Become familiar with some words which are spelled with **ai** to make the long /a/ sound.

   ┌─────────────────────────────────────┐
   │ **Spelling Tip**   │
   │ Some words that make the long   │
   │ /a/ sound are spelled **ai**.   │
   └─────────────────────────────────────┘

   Copy the words and underline **ai**. Say the words aloud as you write them.

   | restrained | chain | train | attain |
   | hair | pair | braid | rain |

2. a. In Lesson 12, you learned how to write and punctuate quotations. Look at the literature passage. The passage is written in three paragraphs. In the first paragraph, Amos Fortune is speaking. In the second paragraph, someone else is speaking. And then in the third paragraph, Amos Fortune speaks again. When using quotations, begin a new paragraph every time a different person speaks.

   b. Write a dialogue between yourself and another student. It can be made up or real. Have each person speak at least two times. Remember to begin a new paragraph every time a new person speaks. If you need to review quotations, refer to the Quotation Rules in Lesson 12.

3.
a. Answers will vary.

3. a. A **fact** is something that can be observed, measured, or proven to be true.
   Ex: It is two miles from here to the store. (Fact)
         We had warm, sunny weather today. (Fact)

   Write a sentence that states a fact.

   b. An **opinion** is a statement that tells what we think or feel about something.
   Ex: I liked the book about dogs the best. (Opinion)
         Hamburgers taste better than hot dogs. (Opinion)

   Write a sentence that states an opinion.

b. Answers will vary.

   c. Use the *Student Activity Book* page 280, or fold a piece of paper in half vertically. (See diagram.)

Fact	Opinion

   Write the words "Fact" and "Opinion" on the top of each column. List at least four facts and opinions about yourself and the things you like or dislike.

   Ex:
   Fact   **Opinion**
   I play baseball.   Baseball is the most exciting sport.

d. Newspapers are an excellent source of facts and opinions. Together with your teacher, look through some newspaper articles for facts and opinions. Some of the words that signal opinions are: think, believe, feel, want, should. Point out at least three facts and three opinions. Advertisements are a great source of opinions.

4.

a. Bill Smith was born in America.

4. a. **Analogies** show how two things relate to each other. Here is an example of an analogy. You have to figure out what kind of relationship exists between the two sets of things.

Amos Fortune : Africa   Bill Smith : America

We know that Amos was born in Africa, so what do we know now about Bill Smith?

b. An arm is a part of a body. A wheel is part of a car.

b. See if you can tell the relationship between these words:
arm : body   wheel : car

c. 1) one part of many parts that go together to make something bigger
2) younger offspring to parent
3) one part of a whole
4) opposites
5) beings and their homes

c. Analogies are like puzzles. You have to figure out how the pieces fit together. Read these word pairs and write the relationship between the items.

1) tree: forest   house : town
2) cub : lion   daughter : mother
3) branch : tree   tail : cat
4) day : night   dark : light
5) birds : sky   fish : water

d. Here are some incomplete analogies. Try to find out what the relationship is in the first set and fill in an appropriate word in the second set

d. 1) finish
2) car, truck, bike
3) house, building, wall
4) books, etc.
5) hen, rooster

1) sell : buy   begin :
2) nest : bird   garage :
3) board : fence   brick :
4) stars : galaxies   words :
5) kitten : cat   chick :

e. Answers will vary.

e. Try to think of at least two analogies of your own. Write them down.

5. a. Listen as your teacher reads the literature passage for dictation. Do not write as it is read the first time, just listen. Remember, writing from dictation is a skill you acquire with practice, like hitting a baseball. Your first attempts may not be too successful, but as you practice you will become better.

   b. After you listen to the literature passage the second time, write what you have heard. When you have finished, compare your copy to the literature passage.

   c. Take a spelling test.

   d. Optional: Choose skills from the *Review Activities* on the next page.

Review Activities

Choose the skills your student needs to review.

1. *Quotations*

   When writing quotations, what do you do every time a new person speaks?

2. *Fact and Opinion*

   a. What is a fact?
   b. What is an opinion?

3. *Analogy*

   a. What is an analogy?
   b. Complete the following analogies.

bird : nest	bear :
shovel : gardener	hammer :
plane : pilot	train :
bread : bakery	money :

---

1. indent

2.
a. A fact is something that can be observed or proven to be true.
b. An opinion is a statement that tells what one thinks about something.

3.
a. An analogy shows how two things relate to each other.
b. bear: den
   hammer: carpenter
   train: conductor
   money: bank

Assessment 6
(Lessons 29 - 32)

1. Complete the sentences with the correct pronoun.

   a. Jamie and (me, I) played softball.
   b. The dog chased Steve and (me, I).
   c. Casey, Paul, and (me, I) went roller blading.

2. What is a biography?

3. Add capitalization.

   a. I will hide god's word in my heart
   b. I trust in god because he loves me.
   c. The lord is good to his people.

4. Look at this word: aimless

   a. What is the base or root word?
   b. What is the suffix?

5. Add punctuation.

   a. My brother was born on August 21 1991.
   b. On September 23 1997 my parents celebrated their twentieth anniversary.
   c. I must return this by May 1 1996.

6. Listed below are guide words from a dictionary. Look at the entry word, and tell if it would be listed on that page.

Guide words	Entry word
a. sample - ship	single
b. brunch - butcher	brother
c. glad - ground	gold

7. How do you begin a new quotation every time a different person speaks?

1.
a. Jamie ad I played softball.
b. The dog chased Steve and me.
c. Casey, Paul and I went rollerblading.

2. A story written about someone.

3.
a. I will hide God's Word in my heart.
b. I trust in God because He loves me.
c. The Lord is good to His people.

4.
a. aim
b. less

5.
a. My brother was born on August 21, 1991.
b. On September 23, 1997 my parents celebrated their twentieth anniversary.
c. I must return this by May 1, 1996.

6.
a. no
b. no
c. yes

7. indent

8. Something that is true, that can be proven

9. Something one feels about soomething; a judgement

10.
a. foot
b. horse
c. cat

8. What is a fact?

9. What is an opinion?

10. Complete these analogies.

a. finger : hand   toe :
b. cub : bear   foal :
c. bark : dog   meow :

BOOK STUDY

on
Caddie Woodlawn

Skills

Vocabulary
Reading Comprehension
Compare and Contrast

Caddie Woodlawn
Written by Carol Ryrie Brinl
Published by Macmillan
Readability - 6th grade

Introducing
Caddie Woodlawn

Spark:
Has your grandmother ever told you stories about her youth? They are fun and interesting to hear! Author Carol Ryrie Brink loved to listen to the true stories her Gram shared and recorded them in *Caddie Woodlawn*. You will read about the red-haired tomboy who lived in Wisconsin at the height of the Civil War.

Summary

Caddie is an eleven year old red-headed tomboy growing up in Wisconsin during the Civil War. She lives happily with her six brothers and sisters and spends most of her time running wild with her brothers Tom and Warren. Her father is the master mechanic at the mill in town, and he seems to understand and appreciate her adventurous spirit. Her mother vainly implores Caddie to be a lady.

Caddie learns many lessons about love, courage, and growing up. She learns about love when she spends her entire silver dollar for some unfortunate children. She learns about courage by finding her friend, Indian John, to warn him of an unjust attack. Finally, when her refined cousin Annabelle comes to visit from Boston, she learns some very hard lessons about growing up. Through her father's tenderness and wisdom, she discovers that growing into a lady is perhaps a fine thing after all.

Father receives news of an inheritance due him in England. The family must decide whether to forsake all they have worked so hard for in America, or forsake the splendid life of nobility in England. At first, the decision seems simple, but when each family member places their vote, they discover that America is their home.

Vocabulary

Find the word in its context. Reread the sentences before and after the word. Do you understand the meaning of the word? Now, look up the word in the dictionary and write a clear, simple definition, and use it in a sentence.

1. perilous (Chapter III)

2. adjustments (Chapter VI1)

3. consult (Chapter XI)

4. gruesome (Chapter XV)

5. comply (Chapter XXII)

Complete the following sentences with the correct vocabulary word or write your own sentences using the vocabulary words.

6. After Mr. Woodlawn made some _____ on the clock, it was as good as new.

7. To gain the inheritance, one must _____ with the conditions of the will.

8. The men knew Mr. Woodlawn's friendship with the Indians, so they did not wish to _____ him.

9. The pigeons began their _____ journey south.

10. Katie was brave and agreed to look at the _____ scalpbelt.

1. dangerous

2. changes to correct

3. to seek advice or opinion

4. disgusting

5. to act according to the rules

6. adjustments

7. comply

8. consult

9. perilous

10. gruesome

1. Answers will vary.
2. Obediah rudely placed his legs on Maggie's (Caddie's good friend) desk. When he refused to move, Caddie was indignant and hit Obediah on the shins with a ruler. All at once, Obediah grabbed Caddie's hair, and Tom and Warren jumped up to save her tormentor. Seeing this, Ashur, Obediah's brother, jumped on Tom and they scuffled on the floor. Teacher came in and broke up the fight. Although she was taunted by Obediah, who was much bigger and stronger than she was, she grabbed him and gave him a hard swat on his behind. Obediah was humbled and Teacher was victorious.
3. The men were tired and restless from waiting. They decided it would be best to attack the Indians before the Indians attacked them. Caddie knew that Indian John was their friend and would not attack them, but her father was not there, so she must go and warn them herself.
4. Indian John had given Caddie a scalpbelt to keep for him. The children thought they could make a profit by putting on a Peep Show in the barn for others to come see. Robert

Discussion Questions

Chapters 1-4

1. From what you read about the Woodlawn children, who do you feel most like? Why?

Chapters 5-8

2. Tell me about the schoolroom battle with Obediah Jones.

Chapters 9-12

3. What did Caddie overhear that made her feel so urgent to find Indian John?

Chapters 13-16

4. Tell me about the children's plan for a Peep Show.

Chapters 17-20

5. Who were the two unexpected heroes in chapter 19? Why were they "unexpected" and how were they heroes?

Chapters 21-24

6. Tell me about the big decision the Woodlawn family had to make.

Ireton, one of Father's hired men, came in to scold the children about using a candle in the barn. After the candle was burned out, Robert brought out his banjo and sang with the children. This made the Peep Show better than ever.

5. The two unexpected heroes were Indian John's dog and Obediah Jones. They were "unexpected" heroes because people generally did not think highly of either of them. Indian John's dog saw the fire and tried to get Caddie's attention at the school window. If he hadn't made all that noise no one would have looked outside and seen the fire. Obediah took command of putting out the fire by beating the flames with boards and digging a ditch around the schoolhouse and showing the other boys what to do.

6. The family had to decide whether to go to England and claim their noble inheritance or remain in America. Father asked each family member to vote "Go" or "Stay." Everyone voted "Stay," except Clara, but Clara changed her mind afterward. They realized that this was their home and they were Americans.

Compare and Contrast

In Chapter 22, Father tells the family about the possibility of living in England. Think about what life would be like for the Woodlawns in England and compare it to their lives in America. What things would be different? What things would be same? Find page 288 in the *Student Activity Book* or draw two large overlapping circles like this:

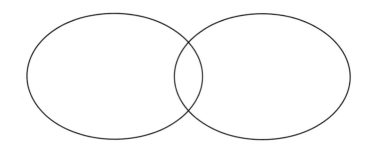

England   America

In the circle labeled England, list what life would be like and do the same with the circle labeled America. Then, in the overlapping area, list the things which would be the same.

I C.A.N. Assessment

for

Caddie Woodlawn - Book Study D

After the *Book Study* is completed, check off each **I C.A.N.** objective with your teacher.

____ **C** I can **complete** my work.

____ I can be **creative**.

____ **A** I can be **accurate**.

____ I can do my work with a good **attitude**.

____ **N** I can do my work **neatly**.

SPEECH MAKING

Skills

Speech to Inform
Speech to Persuade
Speech to Demonstrate
Outline

1- 2.

a. This speech was probably given with much feeling, because of the urgency of the situation.

1. - 2. Have you ever heard a speech? Maybe one of your parents has given a speech, or you've heard a government official give one. During these two weeks you will prepare and present a speech of your own. There are many types of speeches and we are going to learn about three of them.

    a. One type of speech is a speech which is given to **inform**. Listen as your teacher reads the first part of this famous speech given by Winston Churchill in 1940. This speech was given in England before a group of government officials to tell them about a crisis that was upon the country.

Winston Churchill Announces New Administration - 1940

Last Friday evening I received His Majesty's commission to form a new administration. It was the wish of Parliament and the nation that this should include all parties, both those who supported the late Government and also the parties of the Opposition. I have completed the most important part of this task. A War Cabinet has been formed of five Members, representing the unity of the nation. The three party leaders have agreed to serve, either in the War Cabinet or in high executive office. The three fighting services have been filled. It was necessary that this should be done in one single day, on account of the extreme urgency and rigor of events.

    The speaker continues to give facts about the situation in the country and to propose a solution. The part of the speech that you have just read is full of information about the condition of the English government in 1940. Talk to your teacher about the facts included in this speech. Do you think they are given with or without feeling? Why or why not?

    b. The second type of speech is the speech given to **persuade**. Listen as your teacher reads a portion of a speech given 2,000 years ago. The speech was given by Julius Caesar, a famous Roman leader, to a group of government officials called Senators.

Julius Caesar Objects to Illegal Execution of The Captured Conspirators
(63 B.C.)

It is the duty of all men, Roman Senators, in their discussions on subjects that are difficult to decide, to strip themselves of hatred and affection, of revenge and pity. When the mind is clouded with such emotions it cannot easily determine the truth; no man has ever followed these emotions and at the same time made a wise decision. When we exercise our judgement only, that is best. Hatred, revenge, and pity can overpower our thinking and we will lose our good judgement. I could tell you a great many examples of kings and other leaders who made foolish decisions because of their resentment or compassion. I would rather tell you the example of our forefathers and show you how they acted differently than their impulses and emotions. They agreed to act wisely and with sound judgement.

The speaker continues by giving an example of earlier Roman leaders who did not execute their enemies and the good that came from that decision. Julius Caesar is trying to convince the Senators not to execute several men who were found guilty of a crime. Look at this portion of the speech again to see how he tries to persuade the Senators.

1) What does Julius Caesar imply is the Senators' possible difficulty in deciding this issue his way?
2) How does he try to convince them that these strong feelings will not help them make wise decisions?

In order to persuade others of his opinion, Julius Caesar presented facts to back up his opinions. He also used what he saw as his opponents' weaknesses as a basis for calling them to change their minds and follow his plan.

b. 1) The Senators probably have strong feelings about these crimes or criminals. 2) He calls it their "duty" not to follow these emotions. He gives his opinion that emotions only make it harder to use good judgement. He refers to mistakes other leaders made following their emotions and gives a specific example of others who did not follow their emotions.

Historical note: After Julius Caesar's speech to the Senators, Marcus Porcius Cato gave a speech demanding the immediate execution of the criminals. By voicing the fears of the Senators and suggesting that Julius Caesar was merely being political, the Senate called for an immediate execution of the men without a trial. Although called a hero at first for this decision, Cato lived to regret it. He later repented the executing of Roman citizens without a trial and the deed resulted in a ruined political reputation which his enemies used against him for years.

c. The final type of speech is a speech given to **demonstrate** something to an audience.

When you give a speech to demonstrate you show and tell your audience how to do a specific thing. Here are some examples:

How to saddle a horse
How to throw a frisbee
How to shoot a basketball
How to separate an egg
How to complete a simple craft project

Listen as your teacher reads the speech entitled *How to Open a Door*.

How to Open a Door

Doors are important to all of us. They help us feel safe; they keep out the rain; and they provide privacy. Sometimes, however, we need to change the position of a door from being closed to being open. Today, I am going to show you the proper way to open one of these fabulous inventions.

The first step is to walk up to the door. You must be closer than an arm's length to properly follow these steps. (Speaker walks to the demonstration door and extends arm.)

The second step is to firmly grasp the door knob. A firm grip ensures success in the next phase of door opening. (Speaker grasps door knob.)

Now turn the door knob using wrist action to complete the turn. (Speaker turns the knob.)

The final step has a bit of a twist to it, as each door has its own manner of opening. You must determine the type of door with which you are working in order to complete this final phase. Either push or pull the door to open it. (Speaker opens the demonstration door.)

As you can see, the door is open now and people can easily pass through it. I hope you will follow these simple steps the next time you need to change the position of a door in your home. And don't forget to be thankful for these very useful items in our lives.

Let's review the three types of speeches:

1) **Speech to inform**: gives facts and information about an event or a person.
2) **Speech to persuade**: tries to convince the audience of an opinion by giving facts to support that opinion.
3) **Speech to demonstrate**: shows and tells an audience how to do a specific thing.

3.   You will now begin to prepare your own speech. Discuss with your teacher the following items to help you decide which type of speech to prepare.
1. Who will be my audience?
2. Which type of speech would be best for this audience?
3. Which type of speech would be best for me to prepare?

Once you have decided the type of speech to present, you must choose a **topic** for the speech.

Suggestions:

Speech to Inform	**Speech to Persuade**
• Science Topic	• Any political/social issue
• Social Studies Topic	• More allowance every week
• Family History	• Appeal for a certain
• Bible History	vacation spot this year

Speech to Demonstrate

- How to do any sport or baking
- How to do a craft
- How to draw

4 - 5. After you have decided on a topic for your speech, it is time to think about that topic. Ask yourself these questions:

1) Is the topic too big to talk about in a few minutes?
2) Can I break it down into smaller pieces?

This step in speech making is called "Narrowing Your Topic." It would be hard to make a short speech on the topic "airplanes." That topic is too big. You can, however, make a speech using a model demonstrating how an airplane flies.

When your topic is very specific, you are ready to gather the information you need for your speech.

To gather information you can:

1) Read books and magazines.
2) Talk to anyone who knows about the subject.
3) Watch a video.
4) Think about information you already know.

Make notes on notebook paper as you find the information. You can write words and phrases rather than complete sentences. Just be sure to include all the information you need—don't assume you will remember something you don't write down.

Review Activities

What are the three types of speeches?

1. - 2a. After you have collected your information, you will need to organize it in some manner. Some people like to use an outline for that purpose. This format may be best for a Speech to Demonstrate. Your main points can be your steps and the details will give information for each step. Use the example below or refer to Lesson 22 for a review of outlines.

I. Main Point
    A. Detail #1
    B. Detail #2

II. Main Point
    A. Detail #1
    B. Detail #2

If you are presenting a "Speech to Inform" you may create a wheel diagram such as:

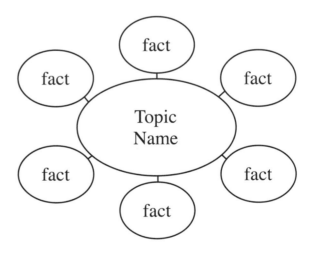

The topic is written in the center and on each spoke is information about the topic. When all your spoke circles are filled, you may want to number them for your presentation.

If you are preparing a "Speech to Persuade" you may use an outline with roman numerals as your opinions and capital letters under each opinion as facts or examples to support your opinion.

  I. Opinion
    A. Fact or example #1
    B. Fact or example #2

  II. Opinion
    A. Fact or example #1
    B. Fact or example #2

There are two very important parts to any speech: the beginning and the ending.

Talk to anyone you know who has given a speech and get suggestions for the beginning of your speech. Suggestions: a joke, appropriate story, question, recent incident, famous quote, or verse.

The ending, or conclusion, of a speech win usually call the audience to some kind of action or response. For example, if you demonstrate how to draw a cat, you may conclude by telling your audience that one day you hope they will try to draw a cat or another animal of interest. A speech on King Richard may conclude by calling the audience to read about their favorite historical figure. A speech on the increasing of an allowance may appeal to the audience to begin this new allowance rate today.

After all your information is gathered and organized, and you have your beginning and ending figured out, you are ready for your final preparations. Either write your speech, or make notes to yourself from which you will present the speech to your audience.

3. - 4. Practice giving your speech at least three times a day. You are not required to memorize the entire passage; however, you should know it well enough to be able to look up from your paper several times during the presentation.

Stand in front of a mirror as you practice. Use the following list to help you evaluate yourself. After you have practiced several times, ask your teacher or another student to evaluate you, using the list.

Oral Presentation Checklist

___ 1.   Do I read slowly?
___ 2.   Do I read clearly?
___ 3.   Do I read loud enough?
___ 4.   Am I using my voice well to communicate the meaning and feeling?
___ 5.   Am I standing up straight, but naturally?
___ 6.   Do I look at my audience enough?

5.   Your presentation day has arrived, and even though you may feel nervous, you are ready for your audience because you planned for it. If you feel very nervous, ask your teacher to sit in the back of the room and give you support by smiling at you.

I C.A.N. Assessment

for

Speech Making Unit

After the *Unit* is completed, check off each **I C.A.N.** objective with your teacher.

C
— I can **complete** my work.

— I can be **creative**.

A
— I can be **accurate**.

— I can do my work with a good **attitude**.

N
— I can do my work **neatly**.

EVERYDAY WORDS

in
"Star-Spangled Banner"

Skills
Memorization
Imagery
Point View
Topic Sentence
Supporting Sentences

The Star-Spangled Banner

(Verse 1)
O say, can you see, by the dawn's early light,
What so proudly we hailed at the twilight's
    last gleaming.
Whose broad stripes and bright stars,
    through the perilous fight,
O'er the ramparts we watched were so
    gallantly streaming!
And the rockets' red glare, the bombs
    bursting in air,
Gave proof through the night that our flag
    was still there:
O say, does that star-spangled banner yet
    wave
O'er the land of the free and the home of the
    brave?

"The Star-Spangled Banner," by Francis Scott Key

Teacher's Note: As your student completes each lesson, choose skills from the Review Activities that he needs. The Review Activities follow each lesson.

1. a. Listen to your teacher read the first verse of "The Star-Spangled Banner" by Francis Scott Key. Though you may have heard this song many times, you may not have been able to understand all the words, or thought about the meaning of each phrase.

   b. Read this verse aloud. Try to read expressively, paying special attention to punctuation marks. Practice reading through this verse several times. Since this is a familiar verse, it should not be difficult to memorize. Work on memorizing this verse this week. If you have a tape recorder, record yourself reading this verse using your most clear and expressive voice.

2. a. Look at the excerpt from the book *Patriotic Songs, Color the Classics* series, entitled "The Star-Spangled Banner." Either read silently, or listen as your teacher reads. Talk with your teacher about the events described. Make a list of these events. You do not need to use complete sentences for your list. You may want to color the picture of the bombardment of Ft. McHenry, also found on page 302 in the *Student Activity Book*.

The Story of "*The Star-Spangled Banner*"
Francis Scott Key
1779-1843

Francis Scott Key lived on a 3000 acre farm called *Tierra Rubra* (Red Land) in Frederick (now called Carroll) County, Maryland. Francis was raised to rely upon God's Word for everything in his life. His mother was instrumental in imparting the Scriptures over everyday issues.

Francis learned much from his blind grandmother. She not only taught Francis to pray, but was also responsible for teaching him to speak in a soft and clear manner. She was the inspiration for his excellent speaking ability which proved to be a tremendous skill for Francis later in life.

Francis studied law under the advice of his uncle Philip. He became the most popular lawyer in Maryland. By the time he was 27 years old, he was in great demand. Francis married the beautiful Mary Taylor Lloyd who gave him 11 children.

By 1814, Britain had been at war with America for two years. Washington D.C. had been captured and burned in August. Later that fall, the British fleet surrounded the Americans in Chesapeake Bay. British Admiral Cochrane had informed secretary Monroe at Fort McHenry, the fort that guarded the narrow entrance into the harbor and secured Baltimore, was about to be destroyed. The British plan was to disable Fort McHenry and then attack Baltimore. Dr. Beanes, a prominent physician and a close friend of Francis Scott Key was captured.

Francis, determined to obtain his friend's release, sought President Madison for the proper paperwork. President Madison knew about Key's persuasive abilities and granted him whatever he needed. Key and Colonel Skinner, sailed under a flag of truce to the *Tonnant*, the admiral's ship. Once on board, Key requested the release of the doctor. Within minutes, Key realized he had chosen the wrong day. This was the day that Admiral Cochrane had selected to attack Fort McHenry. Cochrane refused to return the physician, Francis Key or Colonel Skinner before the planned attack.

Admiral Cochrane received bad news. His land forces attacking the city had been driven back with many casualties. He was told that unless Fort McHenry was captured or completely destroyed, the whole campaign would be lost.

The news that this crusade would soon be lost was followed by fierce bombardment. The shelling started at daybreak on the 13th of September, 1814 and continued through the night. Sixteen British frigates took part in the bombing. Fifteen to eighteen hundred rounds were fired. It was a tiresome night. Key, Skinner and Dr. Beanes anxiously waited as they watched the attack.

Key had been told by British sailors to take a good look at his precious flag because it would not be there by morning. Key could not take his eyes off the fort which was attacked by land and by sea. The disheartened Americans were desperately trying to retaliate but the 42-pound cannons could not reach the British ships. Cannon ball after cannon ball left the American fort only to dive straight into the water before the fleet. Admiral Cochrane was quite confident that the fort would be taken easily. He was anxious to finish off this job so that he could destroy the rest of Maryland.

By early morning there was great silence and Key was slowly giving up hope. Through the smoke of battle and the early morning mist, he grabbed a pair of field glasses and looked toward the fort 2½ miles away. Would the waving flag be American or British? One can only imagine the thoughts that ran through Key's mind. He gasped as he saw the 15-starred flag still waving. The Americans had not surrendered. After the shelling of 1800 rounds, our flag had received 11 holes and only 4 out of 1,000 men died in the fort. When all the smoke had cleared, history recorded that a small poorly-equipped army of men had fought and won against the greatest army and navy in the world.

Francis took a letter from his pocket and quickly jotted down a few stanzas. Having received word of total defeat, the British, had no choice but to return Francis Key, Colonel Skinner and Dr. Beanes back to Maryland. That night, in a local hotel, Key finished his poem. The following morning he showed it to his brother-in-law, Judge Joseph Nicholson, who had been second-in-command at Fort McHenry and lived through the bombardment.

The poem called "The Defense of Fort McHenry," first appeared in the Baltimore newspaper, "American." People liked it and began to sing it to a tune that allegedly came from an old drinking song in England called, "To Anacreon In Heaven." One reason for its popularity was that the colonists already knew the tune. The "Star-Spangled Banner" was not accepted formally as our national anthem until Herbert Hoover signed a law in 1931.

Used by permission from *Color the Patriotic Classics*. One in the series of historical books and musical cassette tapes from *Color the Classics* by Carmen Ziarkowski.

Used by permission from *Color the Patriotic Classics*. One in the series of historical books and musical cassette tapes from *Color the Classics* by Carmen Ziarkowski.

2. b. 1) saluted
      2) shining
      3) cannon
      4) decorated
      5) dangerous
      6) embankment
      7) bravely
      8) explosive
      9) flag
     10) light

3. b.

1) War was declared by the United States in June, 1812 and the Treaty of Ghent was signed in December, 1814. It was fought in America, around the Great Lakes and the Northeast, and on the waterways.

2) The British and French were already at war, and the Americans wanted to maintain trade, but people wanted to side with one country or the other. There also was the desire to acquire land in the North American continent from these countries. All of these factors led to war.

3) The war served to distance Americans from their European ties, to show the need for a strong military and to reinforce the idea that it was not good to become entangled in foreign affairs. It also seemed that negotiation was a better way to settle issues than war.

4) When the Treaty of Ghent was signed no one really won; however, America remained independent of European nations and developed friendly ties.

b. This verse is full of interesting words, images, and thoughts. The colorful language in this verse helps us feel like we were there at Fort McHenry. Read over this list of words. Look up their definitions. Find the meaning that is used in the passage.

1) hailed   6)   rampart
2) gleaming   7)   gallantly
3) rocket   8)   bomb
4) spangled   9)   banner
5) perilous   10)   glare

c. Continue to work on memorizing the verse.

3. a. The bombardment of Ft. McHenry was part of what is known as the War of 1812. Using an encyclopedia, or other reference book, look up the War of 1812.

b. After reading, answer these questions orally during discussion with your teacher.

1) How long did this war last, and where did it take place?
2) What issues were being fought over during the War of 1812?
3) What effect did this war have on America?
4) Who won the war?

c. Here are some terms that became widely used relating to the War of 1812. Look them up in the dictionary and write their meanings.

1) impressment
2) frigate
3) privateer

4. You have read about and discussed the War of 1812. You have also read a brief telling of Francis Scott Key's story about the writing of "The Star-Spangled Banner." Reread the ninth paragraph of the story about "The Star-Spangled Banner" that begins with the sentence, "By early morning ..." on page 264. Imagine that you are witnessing this scene, like the people in the story. Write a paragraph telling how you would feel if you had been there. Events:

1) Morning has come.
2) You look at the fort.
3) You see the American flag still waving.

5. One of the most important things a writer does to make poetry special is to create **imagery** for us. An image consists of words that make us see pictures in our minds. Along with the picture, the poet might also provide something to hear, taste, smell, or feel. Images are the special effects of poetry. They help us understand the poem by helping us experience it.

Make two lists of images from verse one of "The Star-Spangled Banner."

1) First, list all the words and phrases you can find that describe the battle.
2) Secondly, list all the words and phrases that describe our flag.
3) Look again at the images describing the battle scene. Orally, describe the whole battle as best you can by concentrating on the images.

c.
1) the forcing of men to serve in the army or navy
2) a warship
3) a privately owned armed ship

4. Answers will vary.

✏ Teacher's Note: You may use the following to spark discussion.

a. Describe the ramparts.
b. How did the American soldiers feel behind those ramparts?
c. Where were the British?
d. What weapons did the British have for firing rockets and bombs?
e. Could the bombs go over the ramparts into the fort? What makes you think so?
f. Did the British have many bombs, or just a few?
g. Why was it such a perilous fight?
h. In addition to what they saw, what did the soldiers hear, smell, taste, feel?

5.
1) perilous fight, ramparts, rockets' red glare, bombs bursting in air
2) broad stripes, bright stars, gallantly streaming, star-spangled banner, wave
3) Answers will vary.

(Verse 4)

O thus be it ever, when freemen shall stand
Between their loved homes and the war's
*   desolation!*
Blest with victory and peace, may the
*   heaven-rescued land*
Praise the Power that hath made and
*   preserved us a nation.*
Then conquer we must, when our cause it
*   is just,*
And this be our motto: "In God is our trust,"
And the star-spangled banner in triumph
*   shall wave*
O' er the land of the free and the home of
*   the brave!*

"The Star-Spangled Banner," by Francis Scott Key

1. a. Listen as your teacher reads the fourth verse of "The Star-Spangled Banner" by Francis Scott Key. After listening, read the verse silently. Make a list of any unknown words. Make sure you understand the meaning of words such as *desolation, preserved, cause,* and *motto.* Look up the definitions of the words on your list.

   b. Make up a sentence, orally or in writing, using each of the words you defined.

   c. Carefully read this verse aloud. Try to read it expressively, paying special attention to punctuation marks. Practice reading through this verse several times and begin to memorize it. Refer to Lesson 1, Tips for Memorizing Poetry.

   d. The message the poet wants you to understand is called the **content**. Sometimes it is helpful to read the poem very slowly and carefully, to understand its content. In your own words, orally or in writing, explain what verse four says by examining the following parts.

1.

a. Possible Answers:
   desolation - misery
   preserved - kept
   cause - purpose
   motto - saying

b. Answers will vary.

272

1) What do the first two lines mean to you?
2) What do lines three and four tell us?
3) What does line five say, and what does line six add to the meaning of line five?
4) Lines seven and eight make the conclusion that our nation can be free if our attitude toward God is right. What three things does verse four tell us to have in our attitude toward God?

2. - 4.

a. For the next three days, you will work on writing an essay.

You may choose to write an essay explaining why you are glad to be an American. This is called a **personal essay** because it gives your opinion or **point of view**.

Or, you may choose to write an essay reporting information on what you have learned about America.

b. To begin, reread the patriotic poems contained in this book and any notes or paragraphs you have written about America. Look at the questions below and use it as a guide to help you write your essay.

Why I am glad to be an American
1) What privileges do you have as an American?
2) What is your heritage as an American?
3) What are your dreams for being an American?

What I have learned about America
1) How did America get its independence?
2) What sacrifices were made?
3) What principles was America built on?

c. The answers to the questions above will become your topic sentence for paragraphs in your essay. Use a separate sheet of paper for each topic sentence. Remember, a **topic sentence** tells the most important thing about the paragraph.

1.
d. 1) We must go to war so that another country—in this case, England—can't take away our freedom.
2) If we win the war we'll have the blessing of peace, and we will preserve our nation. However, we mustn't forget that God is the one who grants us victory.
3) If we are fighting for the right reasons, then we must do all we can to win. Line six adds that we should always trust in God.
4) We must believe that God is having us fight for a cause that is just. We must trust in Him. We must thank Him for the victory.

d. After each topic sentence, write two or three sentences giving details of your topic sentence or reasons why your topic sentence is true. These sentences are called **supporting sentences**. You have now written paragraphs. These paragraphs will make up the body of your essay.

e. The introduction to your essay should tell your reader what the essay is about and capture your reader's attention so he will want to read the rest of your paper. On a separate sheet of paper, write the **introductory paragraph** in three or more sentences.

f. Your **closing paragraph** will connect the main points of the body of your essay. This conclusion will also tell your reader why it was important for you to write this essay. On a separate sheet of paper, write three or more sentences concluding your essay.

g. You should have at least five sheets of paper. Put them in order with the introductory paragraph first, the body paragraphs next, and the closing paragraph last. This is the rough draft of your essay. Reread it and edit your writing as needed. Ask your teacher to check your work for spelling and punctuation.

h. When you are satisfied with your writing, rewrite or type the final version of your essay on one or two pieces of paper, making sure the paragraphs are in the correct order.

5. a. Present your essay to your family or class. You may also want to present dramatic readings of other stories or poems, presentations from memory or songs concerning America. There are many ways to make this presentation a special event—such as inviting other family members to contribute, making and serving refreshments, videotaping this presentation, or including drama.

b. Optional: Recite the first or fourth verse of "The Star-Spangled Banner."

Enrichment Answers

The Enrichment Activities answers are listed below. Since the Enrichment Activities are not numbered, you can easily locate them by the Lesson number that proceeds it in the *Student Activity Book*. Some of the Enrichment Activities do not have a specific answer. For those, please read the directions in your student's book and evaluate the activity accordingly.

Farmer Boy Book Study A - Discussion Questions
  1. reaping
  2. geranium
  3. apprentice
  4. petrified
  5. cultivate

Lesson 1, 2e.
    Answers will vary.

Lesson 2, 5f.
    Possible answers :
    1. glass, jar   4. glass, board
    2. baby, man   5. car, window
    3. door, box   6. sister, man

Lesson 2, 3e
    Possible answers :
    1. hair   2. fight   3. coat   4. pot   5. tent

Lesson 2, 5c.
    Answers will vary.

Lesson 3, 3h

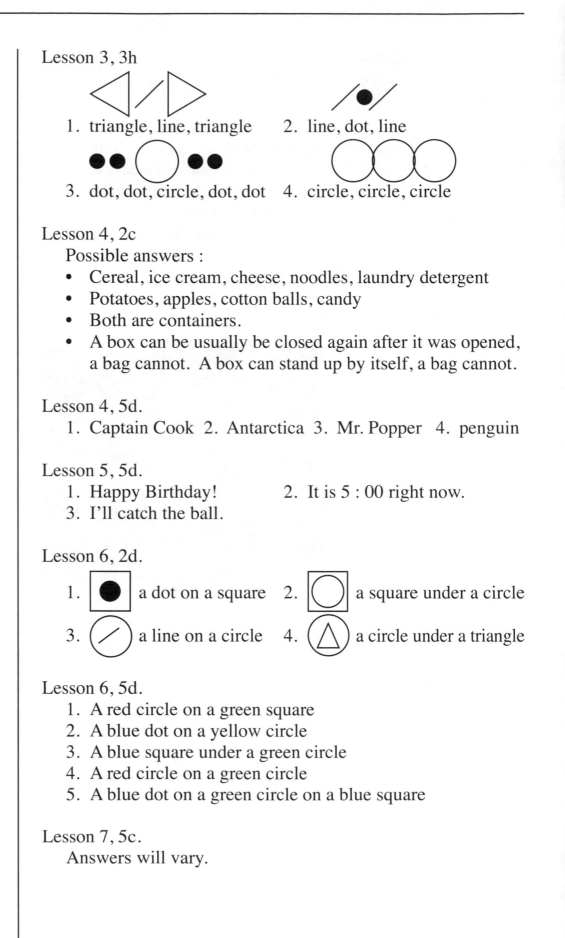

1. triangle, line, triangle   2. line, dot, line

3. dot, dot, circle, dot, dot   4. circle, circle, circle

Lesson 4, 2c
Possible answers :
- Cereal, ice cream, cheese, noodles, laundry detergent
- Potatoes, apples, cotton balls, candy
- Both are containers.
- A box can be usually be closed again after it was opened, a bag cannot. A box can stand up by itself, a bag cannot.

Lesson 4, 5d.
1. Captain Cook 2. Antarctica 3. Mr. Popper 4. penguin

Lesson 5, 5d.
1. Happy Birthday!   2. It is 5 : 00 right now.
3. I'll catch the ball.

Lesson 6, 2d.
1. a dot on a square 2. a square under a circle
3. a line on a circle 4. a circle under a triangle

Lesson 6, 5d.
1. A red circle on a green square
2. A blue dot on a yellow circle
3. A blue square under a green circle
4. A red circle on a green circle
5. A blue dot on a green circle on a blue square

Lesson 7, 5c.
Answers will vary.

Lesson 8, 3 and 4
1. A comb is not a piece of clothing.
2. A tiger is not a reptile.
3. Shoes are not a part of the body.
4. Fruit is not a color.

Lesson 8, 5
1. animal, cat, pet
2. transportation, vehicle, van
3. clothes, hat, baseball cap
4. food, dinner, spaghetti

Lesson 9, 2c.
1. book, novel, *Strawberry Girl*
2. food, snack, cookie
3. food, fruit, apple
4. plant, tree, oak

Lessons 10&11, 5
1. Nouns : frog, man, car
   Verbs : jump, run, jog
2. Parts of a hand : finger, thumb, palm
   Parts of a foot : toe, heel, sole
3. Clothes : jacket, shirt, shorts
   Foot wear : boots, sneakers, slippers

Trumpet of the Swan Book Study
Word Search
 trumpet
 swan
 louis
 debt
 serena

```
r h i s d s d e b t
c t s e r e n a i n
o r o m o u o l p t
n u c t r z m o l e
c m h r h z h u p l
r p a a a l s i a p
e e i m i e t s i u
t t k s w a n l j o
e a c i n c r e t c
```

Lesson 12, 2d.
1. land animals : mouse, snake, lion
   water animals : shark, flounder, whale
2. food : sandwich, cracker, cookie
   drinks : hot chocolate, tea, juice
3. land transportation : bulldozer, tracker, taxi
   air transportation : helicopter, airplane, jet

Lesson 12, 5d.
Word Search
  well
  oh my
  dear
  wow

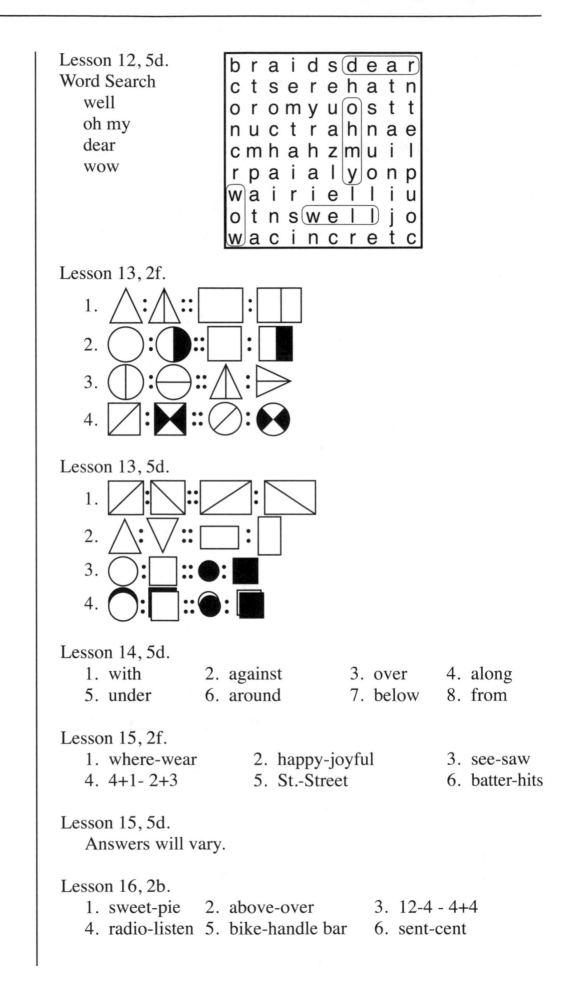

Lesson 13, 2f.

Lesson 13, 5d.

Lesson 14, 5d.

1. with   2. against   3. over   4. along
5. under   6. around   7. below   8. from

Lesson 15, 2f.

1. where-wear   2. happy-joyful   3. see-saw
4. 4+1- 2+3   5. St.-Street   6. batter-hits

Lesson 15, 5d.
Answers will vary.

Lesson 16, 2b.

1. sweet-pie   2. above-over   3. 12-4 - 4+4
4. radio-listen 5. bike-handle bar   6. sent-cent

Lesson 16, 5g.
1. They are opposites.
2. An eye can wink.
3. A seed is part of an apple.
4. They are synonyms.
5. They are opposites.
6. They are synonyms.

Lesson 17, 3e.
1. two   They are synonyms.
2. swam   The second word is the past tense of the first.
3. truck   The first word is a part of the second word.
4. 4x4   The second set equals the first number.
5. thick   They are synonyms.
6. 2+2   The first set equals the second set.

Lesson 17, 5c.
1. never   They are opposites.
2. neigh   The second word is the sound the first one makes.
3. try The first word is the past tense of the second word.
4. fly The second word is what the first one can do.
5. subtract   They are synonyms.
6. blue   They are homonyms.

Lesson 18, 3e.
   Answers will vary.

Lesson 18, 5d.
   Answers will vary.

Lesson 19, 2d.
   Answers will vary.

Lesson 19, 5d.

1. talking on the phone   2. brushing teeth

3. playing basketball   2. pushing a cart   5. playing baseball

Lesson 20, 2d.
Answers will vary.

Lesson 20, 5d.
Answers will vary.

Lesson 21, 2f.

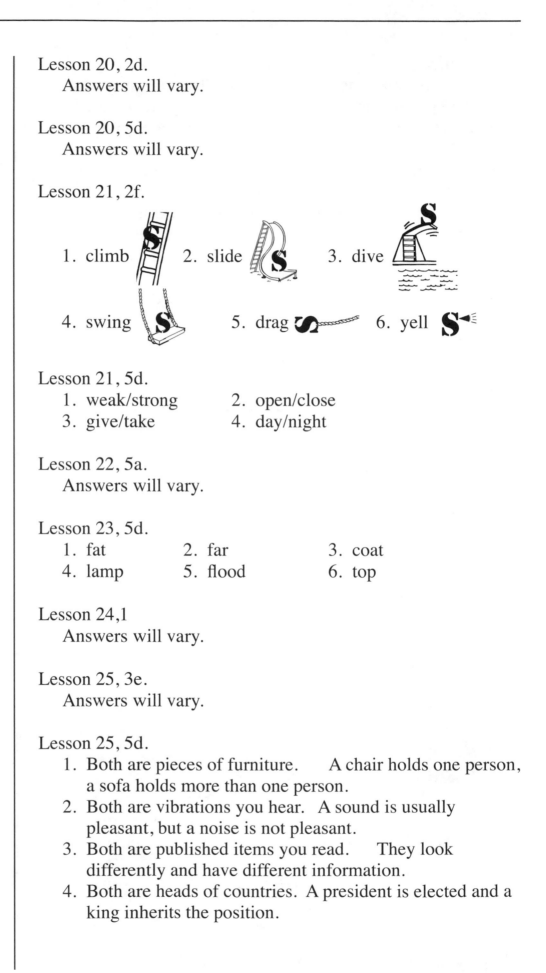

1. climb   2. slide   3. dive

4. swing   5. drag   6. yell

Lesson 21, 5d.
1. weak/strong   2. open/close
3. give/take   4. day/night

Lesson 22, 5a.
Answers will vary.

Lesson 23, 5d.
1. fat   2. far   3. coat
4. lamp   5. flood   6. top

Lesson 24, 1
Answers will vary.

Lesson 25, 3e.
Answers will vary.

Lesson 25, 5d.
1. Both are pieces of furniture.   A chair holds one person, a sofa holds more than one person.
2. Both are vibrations you hear. A sound is usually pleasant, but a noise is not pleasant.
3. Both are published items you read.   They look differently and have different information.
4. Both are heads of countries. A president is elected and a king inherits the position.

Lesson 26, 2e.
1. Both are parts of a plant. A root is below ground and a stem is above the ground.
2. Both are clothing you wear. A uniform is like everyone else's in the group, a suit is not.
3. Both are outside ball games. Baseball uses equipment for moving the ball, soccer does not.
4. Both are eating utensils. A spoon holds food, a fork stabs it.

Lesson 26, 5d.
Answers

Lesson 27,
1. Healthy can describe athlete.
2. Both equal 2.
3. They are homonyms.
4. Went is the past tense of go.
5. Both equal 16.
6. Sharp can describe knife.

Lesson 28, 3b.
1. collapsed   2. trickled   3. trudged
4. pounded   5. whimpered   6. grinned

Lesson 28, 5d.
Answers will vary.

Lesson 29, 2c.
Answers will vary.

Lesson 29, 5d.

1. square, square, square

2. line, line, circle

3. dot, line, circle, line, dot

4. triangle, square, triangle

Lesson 30, 5d.
Answers will vary.

Lesson 31, 3b.
    Answers will vary.

Lesson 32, 2b.
    train
    hair
    braid
    attain
    parr
    chain

Lesson 32, 5d.
    Answers will vary.

Caddie Woodlawn Book Study D
    Answers will vary.

```
b r a i d s d e a t
c t s e r e n a t n
o r o m o u o s t t
n u c t r a i n a e
c m h a h z h u i l
r p a i a l p o n p
h a i r i e a l i u
t t n s w a i l j o
e a c i n c r e t c
```

Skills Index

The numbers and letters listed after each skill refer to the Lesson number and Book Study.

Book Studies:
Farmer Boy -A
Trumpet of the Swan - B
Number the Stars - C
Caddie Woodlawn - D

Composition

Brainstorming - 10, 11
Character Sketch - 23
Closing Paragraph - 36
Creative Writing - 3, 4, 6, 7, 10, 11, 13, 18, 35
Descriptive Sentences - 4, 16, 21
Dialogue - 12, 20, 32
Dictation - 3-7, 12-15, 18-22, 25-32
Directions - 24
Envelope - 5
Essay Writing - 36
Fragment - 3
Friendly Letter - 5, 15
Illustrating - 2, 9, 10, 11, 16
Imagery - 35
Indent - 3, 4, 7, 18

Introductory Paragraph - 36
Lists - 1, 2, 4, 9, 10, 11, 12, 16, 32, 35
Negative Words - 6
Newspaper Article - 6
Oral Presentation - 8, 10, 11, 22, 26, 34
Outlines - 24, 34
Paragraphs - 3, 4, 7, 10, 11, 20, 23, 24, 32, 35, 36
Poetry - 2, 4, 16
Point of View - 36
Report - 6, 7
Sentences - 3, 6, 16, 28
Speech - 33
Supporting Sentence - 7, 18, 36
Topic - 3, 7, 10, 11, 18, 23

Grammar

Study Skills

Reading

Spelling

Literature Used in Book Studies

Brink, Carol Ryrie. *Caddie Woodlawn*. New York: Macmillan Publishing.

Lowry, Lois. *Number the Stars*. Boston: HMH Books for Young Readers.

White, E.B. *The Trumpet of the Swan*. New York: Harper Collins Publishers.

Wilder, Laura Ingalls. *Farmer Boy*. New York: Harper and Row Publishers.

See where learning takes you.

www.commonsensepress.com

Congratulations,
You Are Part Of The *Common Sense Press* Family.

Now you can receive our FREE e-mail newsletter, containing:
- Teaching Tips
- Product Announcements
- Helpful Hints from Veteran Homeschoolers
- & Much More!

Please take a moment to register with us.

Common Sense Press
Product Registration
8786 Highway 21
Melrose, FL 32666

Or online at
www.commonsensepress.com/register

After registering, search our site for teaching tips, product information, and ways to get more from your *Common Sense Press* purchase.

Your Name _____

Your E-Mail Address _____

Your Address _____

City _____ State _____ Zip_____

Product Purchased _____

From What Company Did You Purchase This Product? _____

Get involved with the *Common Sense Press* community.
Visit our web site to contribute your ideas, read how others
are teaching their children, see new teaching tips, and more.